# EXACTING CLAM No. 14 — Autumn 2024

MW01259997

## CONTENTS

Front cover: "Cafés of Desire" by John Patrick Higgins
Interior art: Jake Goldsmith, Nicole Ricci, Walter Smart
© 2024 Sagging Meniscus Press
All Rights Reserved
ISBN: 978-1-963846-23-2
exactingclam.com
Exacting Clam is a quarterly publication from Sagging Meniscus.

Contributing Editors: Jake Goldsmith, Tomoé Hill, Kurt Luchs, Melissa McCarthy, M.J. Nicholls, Mike Silverton, Thomas Walton
Contributing Metaclamician: Christopher Boucher
Senior Editors: Jeff Chon, Elizabeth Cooperman, Tyler C. Gore, Doug Nufer
Fiction Editor: Charles Holdefer · Poetry Editor: Aaron Anstett · Reviews Editor: Jesi Bender
Assistant Editor: Rayne Haas
Editorial Interns: Nina Mazariegos, Nora Schobel
Executive Editor: Guillermo Stitch
Publisher: Jacob Smullyan

Melissa McCarthy

# Orcas and/or Authors

## In the ocean

Last summer my favourite marine-related newspaper headline was about the orca. Formerly known as the killer whale, blackfish, grampus, it's a toothed whale, so, a mammal, of the dolphin family. A cosmopolitan species, says the online encyclopedia, which sounds positive, but the description goes on to explain that the name of the genus, *Orcidus*, means 'from the kingdom of the dead.' Which is more ominous.

There was a glut, a shoal, of oceanic-creature news last year: Sweden suspected a beluga whale of being a Russian spy. Footballer Martin Øde-gaard won a fish (this was actually in September 2019, when he was Real Sociedad's player of the month, but I didn't notice until later). It was feared that Floridian cocaine sharks might be feasting on abandoned drugs. Anchovies advanced our understanding of fluid motion physics by creating turbulence in water temperature while having sex.

All good, but the best, for me, was the UK *Guardian*'s report on orcas in the Bay of Biscay, the headline of which read, "Whales are ramming boats—but are they inspired by revenge, grief or memory?" It's an entertaining article, in which the journalist, Emma Beddington, explains some science while taking pleasure in the inherent absurdity of the situation, in the attributing of human, grand-scale emotions to animals, as though they too partake of The Drama. But I became stranded on just the headline, with its strangely tempting question. Revenge, grief, or memory—or what else might be the orcas' motivation? The usual suspects: hunger or fear; money, power, sex; jealousy, desire. Or maybe they are reprobate teenage orcas, who do it for fun: smash boats, steal motors, just for the halibut.

## On the screen

The phrasing also reminded me of a detail from an artwork that I spend a lot of time poring over: it's *Jaws,* the film of 1975, and in particular the scene where Police Chief Brody is shown typing out the death report for a young woman who has been eaten by a shark. It must be a requirement for the police department, or the coroner's office, perhaps—some sort of admin for the kingdom of the dead. (The skinny-dipping character is Chrissie Watkins, played by Susan Backlinie, who has recently died for real in May 2024; her obituaries can be read in the *New York Times* and other archives.) The fictional death report page, with its boxes, category headings, and spaces to type, is great. Some of the sections are unsurprising: date, deceased's occupation, investigative division. Then it has the excellent section

PROBABLE CAUSE OF DEATH

followed by, in the next box,

REASON: Quarrel—illness—revenge, etc

I don't see many (any) death reports in the normal course of things, so I don't know whether this is the normal language and phrasing for one, or whether Spielberg's props designer thought, correctly, that this would be effective. But it's puzzling, too. I can see the potential for drawing a distinction between a cause of death and a reason—one the immediate, proximate occurrence from a range of possible options; the other, a more subtle interpretation of various forces that led up to the event? But these prompts are rather medieval in tone. Quarrel, illness, revenge; why not the full set of plague, heresy, jousting accident? Though the mention of revenge is also very Greek tragedy-esque, which suggests another motive for the orcas, back in real life: divine instruction or inspiration, embodying or delivering a message from the gods. Obeying the oracle through the spiracle.

Brody in the film reluctantly types in 'SHARK ATTACK' as the CAUSE. But he doesn't get a chance to fill in the next, REASON, box, not with any of the options, because a phone call comes in telling him (we'll learn) that there's been another. This REASON field, as far as we the audience ever witness, remains blank, unstruck by the uprising metal keyslugs.

## On the Page

So my interest was hooked by these two questions, one from the newspaper, one from the cinema: what is inspiring the orcas; and, what is the reason for Chrissie's shark-death? You can see that although they have thematic similarities, the former is a more direct question, simply asking, why are they doing this. In the second scenario, of *Jaws* the film and preceding year's book, Brody has a more complex problem posed to him, as he's asked to discern not just what has happened, but why—the cause and reason—and furthermore, what he should do about it. He's required to do fact-finding, piecing together, interpretation, hypothesizing, dissection, explanation, negotiation, planning. It's a lot more to unfold than in the orca investigation, with its simple 'This. Why?'

And, as I'm literarily-inclined, the two questions put me in mind of Richard Scarry's 1968 classic, *What Do People Do All Day?*, which is a large-format, illustrated book introducing children to the idea of careers, day-time activity, in fact to the whole concept that there is a broader world out there. Which is at the heart of much literature. (1968 was a good year in our field of publication; P.K. Dick's *Do Androids Dream Of Electric Sheep?*, Judith Kerr's *The Tiger Who Came To Tea*, and Scarry's own *The Supermarket Mystery* all date from then too.) I admire the expansive concept of the book, and the directness of its title, and the way that the contents, in simple words and hugely detailed drawings, answer the question. Also, Scarry takes the word 'people' on his own terms, expanding it to include worms, pigs, rabbits, and all. It strikes me, though, that we're missing the sequel. Scarry tells us 'what,' but leaves out the 'why.' And this is the task that the newspaper article, and Brody, and now, I feel, I too, all edge towards: explaining not only, what do people do all day; but also, why do they do that.

It's hard, as we've seen, to answer this for orcas. But it's also hard to answer it for anybody, in any sphere or genus. Brody at his typewriter. Me at my desk—writing, that's the main thing I do. The question starts to come back and bother me, as though I'm a Spanish fisherman hearing an unnerving, repetitive thumping against the hull, a problem under the waterline that won't leave me alone. Why do orcas and/or writers do that?

## On the Pitch

Maybe I should start with something easier, something that is my second-most-frequent activity: playing football (I live in Scotland: soccer.) Why do football players do those things they do? It seems like an easy question. The easy answer is that they're trying to manoeuvre the ball in order to score more goals than the other side. But it's not that, exactly. Or, it's not that, the way I play it.

Football, instead, is about movement through time and over distance (minutes and leagues), and about understanding and anticipating how other people's thoughts will prompt their bodies to move, and about shaping patterns over a space that's confined by lines and by rules. The ball is incidental; it's not the object, the point of the game. Why does a player do that thing? Because they've seen the space and trajectory, and the moment, that's about to open up. Because they've caught my eye and know where I'm about to run. Because they've got a grudge to assuage against that other player. Because a teammate is shouting at them to go somewhere, do something, refrain from something (sometimes all of these at once, with swearing). Because it brings them delight to make the ball circle overhead like that. There are constraints, but within them, there's the creative freedom to read what is happening and to dream up a response, that will get you where you want to go. Reshaping, speeding up, reducing to freeze-frame clarity at moments of excitement and emotion. Starting again. Trying again better. And it's about thinking, about being in mental sympathy with your team and opponents. Imaginatively considering the position of the other, in the shared space.

It's a game of geometry through time, every time. A line becomes clear to you, that you could take. But the trajectory is not plot-able, predict-able, on account of all of the other people on the pitch who are all doing their own differently-motivated thing. The obstacles, defenders, challenges, don't stand still but move constantly, so the problem shifts as you look at it and move through it. The network expands with every movement and decision of every node, or, player, within it. An explosion of complexity.

I'm reminded of the story about the French philosopher Derrida coming back from the tea-break to deliver the second half of a lecture that, somewhat to the confusion of his listeners, had seemed to be largely about swirling unpre-dictability, plus dairy and bovine matters. "They tell me," he clarified, "that it's actually pronounced KAY-oss. Not cows." I mention this because this seems to be turning into an essay about the human/animal interface, even though I'm deeply bored by the whole beyond-the-human, thinking-with-animals strand of rumination. I like to do thinking with books. Or on my feet.

## In the study

What about writers, why do they do that thing they do? What decisions are they taking, why do they put down those words in this way not another? Same as footballers, they chose their constraints—format, language, genre, person, register, vocabulary, words, words, words—then they do whatever they want or can within that. They imaginatively consider the position of the other, in the shared space (that's an action replay). They go outside the lines sometimes. But why? It could be that the writer is trying to tackle ideas around imagining people in places,

through time; is considering past motive, future possibilities, the immediate texture and sensation of the present moment; is shaping patterns through memory. Trying to trap, control, turn these ideas then send them. (And all of this consideration is aside from the reply that director Hitchcock reportedly gave to an actress asking about her motivation: "It's the money, my dear.")

Though I'm drifting more towards another answer, too, one which is prompted by the example of the footballer who does it for fun, for the jouissance of just mucking about and fooling around. The writer writes that thing because there's an inexplicable pleasure in doing so and a compulsion towards it. Much as it pains me to admit it, (because they're my second-least-favourite marine animal, next to your straight-up dolphin), maybe the writer and the orca are doing similar things: just expressing their thoughts through action in the best way, because it's in their nature. That's what the writer has, the call of the mild. And there's not just a parallel, but a triangular symmetry between the footballer, the writer, and the orca. They all three are in their zones doing their black and white enjoyment.

For example, there's a certain similarity to the classic football ball, in the polygonal, monochrome shaping of the orca's head and body. Aerodynamic, black and white, made of hexagons and pentagons. It bounces around. It bumps into the humans. It looks perhaps friendly until in swims up at thirty-five-plus miles per hour and whacks you. The monochrome, too, reminds me of the issue of negative or complementary space. Figure and ground advancing or receding. Attack, drop back. Splash of white foam over the dark water. White page, black type. Spaces for the words, but they might never, for reasons powering in from the watery kingdom of death, they might never get around to being written.

## Off the Ball

An aspect of the football playing that I wonder if it carries over into the writing, is the idea of the off-the-ball. The game, as I've suggested, is not so much about what you do when you have the ball and kick it. Most of the time, and the point, is spent without: after you've passed, when you're running into space; when you're moving to adjust the overall configuration of the people dispersed over the field, changing the shape. No, the main point in footy is what's *not* happening, or, what's not exactly the main event happening at the place you might expect to be the centre of attention. The main point is everywhere elsewhere, all but the focal point, the eye of the storm.

And the same with the orca—it's not just their actual sinking of the fishing boat that is important, but the whole surrounds to the event, the hinterland or the hinter-watery-bay. Not just the moment of impact but everything around that, the *hors-crash*, too. It's the build-up, the development of the narrative and the aftermath, the questions arising around revenge, grief, memory, desire. Whatever those motivations and feelings were, or might be, or become. The all-around, the medium we swim in. Everything that's connected, all the waiting that we do.

And for the writer, too. Not just the punctum moment, but the everything-else-ness of writing. Yes, it's the chosen word on the page, but it's the rest of the page, and the beyond the margins, the history of the previous stories and everything you're read before, earlier, too. Everything you bring to bear on it. The words and the worlds all around, that you chart your way through, that you navigate in, that count.

## In the Box

Looking back to Brody's form in *Jaws*, it's a request for written information—Brody has to give something over to the authorities by it. But the form is also (and in exchange) imparting in-

formation to him, through its configuration and categories. It's telling Brody and us what aspects of a death, life, and event are already considered pertinent by the issuers of the document, telling us what they think is relevant. What was the CAUSE, asks the form, while putting forwards some of the expected or acceptable answers, pre-framing how to understand events. This is not a blank sheet, open-water space in which to free-associate anything about Chrissie; only certain, curtailed details are called for.

It's the posing of the question that is, itself, part of the answer, really. To ask is already to frame what could go here; a question is a way of setting out important information about the information—marine info, pitch info, textual info—that is being requested. By casting the net out you're already giving a clue about what you think you'll be hauling back in, fetching out of the back of the net. Asking the question, it seems, is also a form of telling, or at very least of clearing a route for, a story to come. It's prepping for an answer, drawing out the white lines of the pitch markings. When you ask you tell; you tell through your questions.

This is what usually happens, an exchange of information back and forth. But this is not, quite, what we get with Brody, and this is why he's my typing and literary hero. The Brody scene is vital because he never does get to the REASON; he's tiki-taka'ing, then a voice summons him and he leaves it blank. Always a blank space, something for us to carry on thinking about filling in with words. Not the moment of the crash of the orca's teeth against the boat, not the moment of the typeslug marking the blank page to record why, not the foot striking the black and white object. But the moments before, and after, rippling around, receding, circling. Spinning out, as far as we can see.

## On the Horizon

What's going to happen this summer? I'll be waiting, watching, ready to run with my reports. If I'm not called away from my typewriter in a hurry, I'll keep readers posted, on what happens. On why? We'll see.

Jake Goldsmith

# Autistic Liberalism

## Confused Meanings and Definitions

Definitions of liberalism are deeply confused—a word, idea, or set of ideas, used in every sense and soon lacking any sense at all. Overuse and confusion can apply to any philosophical idea, political implementation, or popular ideology, but I want to draw particular attention to liberalism and its misuse (without providing a dogmatic definition), rather than socialism, conservatism, etc., all with their own particular follies and all frequently misunderstood.

I risk being rude or intellectually primitive, but I fail to see a consistent or reliable definition of liberalism, in all its varieties, outside niche academic circles. Although it's not really the scope of this piece to provide a comprehensive explanation, liberalism, considered only as a concept, let alone a physical and infrastructural reality, appears more malleable and easily subverted or self-subverted in its motifs or its intentions, than other historical or contemporary political ideas applied to reality. I won't attempt to give some perfect definition here (if that is even possible). And indeed, there are certainly varieties of liberalism that I reject. There are versions of liberalism less hospitable to democracy, noting the strong possibility that wider democratic participation can be reactionary rather than constructive or helpful—which is still in some part an inherent fragility democratic regimes must contend with. Hopefully I can justify my ambivalence to dogmatic definitions later. I want to at least suggest, briefly, an outline of the particular meanings of liberal thought, its inherent vulnerability, and a rejection of varied positivist notions of liberalism and other ideologies. If I detailed every instance of the use of liberalism as a label (many of which are inaccurate or absurd) I could write several volumes, for which reason I only want to write a brief outline of a particular understanding, sharing an ambivalent view of historical epistemology with Raymond Aron and his *Introduction à la philosophie de l'histoire* (*Introduction to the Philosophy of History*, 1938).

Part of this analysis is likely impoverished given my particular reading, and my rejection of popular, contemporary analyses of liberalism in its multiplicity of meanings, analyses of so-called post-liberalism, and a possibly *autistic* focus on history and historical motifs (in short, ideals) with the view that many liberal governments are only nominally liberal; suffering from democratic degeneration and abuses of power that undermine them. I want to avoid common talk where political categories are used pejoratively—and whether one is rightly opposed to something or not, there is little understanding of what any category is or should be. There's often talk in semi-scholarly literature, or more rudely on the internet, of the death of liberalism or of other ideologies. These declarations should be proposed with more acute and deliberate meanings, but often give us obtuse or misleading, contradictory meanings instead. All such meanings and definitions have very personal, individual understandings behind them—political names can be regarded as anything the author wants them to mean without much diligence, depending more on aesthetic dispositions. These often basic or abstract definitions make polemics and critique much easier. Shallow versions of the left, or the centre, or the right can shape language in any fashion—with language being better at describing dreams and emotions than considered thought. It matters if we have silly or outright wrong understandings of what political ideologies are even if we dislike them. How is one meant to be better, or combat what is worse, if we don't attempt to have more cogent (if never perfect) definitions? Many are immune to such teachings no matter what the source, having already made up their minds and become resistant to information. But we have to live with this tension.

Instead of holding consistent aspirations, regimes as well as personal ideas need to be understood as inconsistent and hypocritical. "People have always created history in the name of ideas, but the history they have created has never faithfully reflected their ideas", as Aron said. Some ideas can easily lend themselves to bad interpretations. Simply providing a dictionary would be somewhat of an improvement to reducing misunderstandings, but never sufficiently robust. As a brief example, *economic liberalism* has many dissimilarities, or is antithetical, to liberalism as defined in other senses. Hayek and Keynes, or 21st \-century wealth speculation and the oft-forgotten social concerns of Adam Smith, have a great many differences and are considerably at odds with each other. The decline of social liberalism in the name of runaway economic interest is often lamentable, with its results often very *illiberal* and just as inhumanly bureaucratic as maligned systems of central planning.

## The Inherent Fragility of Liberal Democracy

John Adams said: ". . . democracy never lasts long. It soon wastes, exhausts, and murders itself. There never was a democracy yet that did not commit suicide."

The full quote provides greater pessimism. Since Adams, our liberal democracies, whatever their sins, have had more success and have proved surprisingly resilient. But this lesson, one of an inherent vulnerability, is one we shouldn't forget. Today we risk the degeneration of liberal democracies (nominal or not) for many reasons: through corruption, anti-democratic policies, a crisis of trust in institutions, unregulated technologies, a neo-feudalistic organisation of wealth, the meddling of foreign enemies, and our own weaknesses and irresponsibility.

In the realm of theory, and not only in practice, something integral to liberalism easily undermines it. Broad ideas of conservatism, socialism, communism, monarchism, or fascism, in the realm of theory and intention or in their physical infrastructure, all provide, one might cautiously say, greater *tolerances* or leeway for moral or political aberrations while maintaining themselves. I'm approaching a 'No True Scotsman' notion of political and philosophical concepts which can easily be regarded as cheap. A socialist regime, or a socially and culturally conservative regime, allows for a greater breadth of policy and *illiberal* behaviour without ceasing to be *socialist* or *conservative*. These regimes, or more abstract ideas, can subvert themselves in other ways so that they may not be considered authentic anymore, but the contention here is that it's far easier, due to the constitutive parts of what liberalism should be, for liberalism and liberal democracy to become corrupted and *no longer liberal*. Meaning: it is a far more fragile idea. I think this may be the case, in analysis, whether I am favourable or not to liberalism—while my particular understanding of it is idiosyncratic and likely open to derision.

The separation of powers is not just a safeguard against abuse, but contingent on liberty itself—which cannot exist if not delicately balanced and precariously mediated. Do other regimes care so much about this, or do they require such an easily corrupted balance? Some might, unfortunately, care less about being delicate mediators. Democracy faces the same challenge—a balance which most governments have achieved only imperfectly and are always susceptible to ruin.

## The Tenuous Relationship Between Ideas and Practice

The failures of Stalinism are often regarded as clear failures to correctly interpret inspiring ideas. I would say this is partly—and reasonably—true, but not absolutely true. Contemporaries of Marx, on the Left or otherwise, warned of possible and easy interpretations of Marxist thought that could lead to catastrophe. Kołakowski also proposed this view. It is true and almost obvious that there isn't some direct line from Marx to Stalin (as if Marx ever wanted the USSR). It is rather that though Marx isn't guilty of what came after him, he was in some part responsible by proclaiming prophetic ideas that lend themselves readily to despotism or demagoguery—an unfortunate legacy that was closer to predictable than impossible. Marx was a genius, and a genius economic diagnostician, but as a prophet and moralising historicist his legacy is wearying. It may be more difficult to make the case that the ideas of Montesquieu and Tocqueville would bear such sour fruit; while we cannot discount the possibility that they do. The failures of liberalism or of liberal democracy are not failures of Montesquieu's disposition or motifs, if we are being charitable. Further credence could be given to this idea in that Montesquieu did not offer any utopian visions which soon succumb to prejudice, while others enthusiastically did. It's harder to corrupt cautious warnings of what *might* happen than active calls to change history as part of grand schemes.

The failures of descendent actions are more likely to be at odds with historical intention or ideal intention. I could suggest, much like 19th century abolitionists, that broadly understood Enlightenment ideas of liberty and equality aren't so much bad in themselves; the failure is in that they're inconsistently, hypocritically, and too narrowly applied—that their proponents don't follow their espoused ideas to the letter, or we still haven't found a proper application, if that's ever possible. It's likewise true that overconfidence, or a pseudoscientific justification of one's apparent truth or correctness, can lead to the justification of all sorts of bad behaviour; and historical or contemporary liberals can still easily believe in such outmoded *scientific* and *natural* justifications as much as political Hegelians or Marxists. With any idea, or any proponent of an idea, we must be wary of latent assumptions and historical epistemology. I will not be bold and say that there could ever be a thing like a perfected liberalism where broad ideas of tolerance, civility, liberty, or equality are not perverted by reality, especially given various diffuse weaknesses. An overemphasis on *individualism*, privatisation, deregulation, has produced callous disregard for vulnerable people and neglect for the basic maintenance of public services. Many so-called liberals have enacted hierarchical, even authoritarian, and abusive policies that reek of clear hypocrisy.

Eugenics has been justified as a progressive measure despite its, frankly, evil and fascistic constitution. Fair ideals even with a fairer implementation can still cause unintended consequences and uncomfortable trade-offs, while it is arguably the case that the flaws of liberal democracies are more often instances of *illiberal* behaviour—or egalitarianism, liberty, and justice denied, unachieved, or adulterated by unjust passions or industrial progress. Industrial and technological progress, and the hierarchies they necessitate, produce an unease with equitable principles that might be impossible to soothe, or is at least exhaustingly difficult to mitigate. Other societies, or governments, have less of a problem here—if in the pursuit of technological or economic or technological progress one has fewer misgivings with societal unease and injustice.

There is still something of an *unbridgeable gap* between the memory of past decisions and present-day experiences. With that said, I will be bold in saying the failures of other non-liberal regimes and their infrastructure may, more likely, have a closer but certainly not straightforward relationship to originating ideas. Such gaps between ideas and practice are always present, but not always the same length.

"Specialists are aware of an economist named Marx, richer, more subtle, and more interesting than the author only of 'Capital'. But the useful Marx, so to speak, the one who may have changed the history of the world, is the one who propagated false ideas . . .

". . . As an economist, Marx remains perhaps the richest, the most exciting of his time. As an economist-prophet, as a putative ancestor of Marxism-Leninism, he is an accursed sophist who bears some responsibility for the horrors of the twentieth century."—Raymond Aron, *Memoirs.*

## TELEOLOGY, PHILOSOPHY, AND HISTORY

Whether it's invoked pejoratively, especially when we regard the crimes and mistakes of contemporary *neoliberalism*, or defined favourably, it's difficult to say liberalism, or the broadest understanding of an egalitarian ideal, has been truly achieved. Is this an audacious statement? The thinker I am most fond of, Raymond Aron, is atypical of some negative or positive understandings of liberalism, especially after his death, and it's easy for me to contend that so-called liberal democracies, especially since the 1980s and 1990s, have not heeded Aronian warnings of their own vulnerability and the possibility of decline. Like Aron I don't find easy comfort in any political orthodoxy, and I am endlessly critical of liberal regimes, while I don't accept their enemies. The further development of neoliberal ideas in the post-Soviet era has suffered similar mistakes to past socialist ideas: a type of teleological arrogance. Meaning, an implicit Fukuyama-esque notion—that their ideas, given a false confidence after the fall of their rival, have the vibe of historical inevitability, narratological victory, or obviousness.

We shouldn't blame Francis Fukuyama so much individually for the supposed inaccuracy of his ideas, or *strawman* him (it's not as if he is some primary influence on world governments), but we can note the lamentable techno-optimism to which he gave a more acute and explicit expression. The so-called and much derided 'End of History' (of the post-1989 order), with a misplaced optimism about its own health and underestimation of anti-democratic forces, is foolhardy. That is in no way an original critique, but continued criticism of these attitudes, well-defined or ill-defined, is warranted. What's known as *reactionary*, or populist, is not some aberration but a consequence of neoliberal hubris—even if its thinking and its methods are a foolish and counterproductive way to react to such arrogance. Democratic degeneration, or illiberal beliefs and policy, result from the weaknesses, crimes, and mistakes of nominally democratic regimes—not just from nefarious foreign interventions or outside prejudice. This doesn't mean we must fear total democratic collapse, but we should be watchful of such degradation and take responsibility for our own weaknesses.

Truthfully I'm not here to defend liberalism *per se* but a particular instance of it. I regard *teleological* liberalism, or a positivist liberalism, or the thought that a philosophy or political approach has a metaphysical, divine, mechanical, spiritual, or natural inclination to becoming dominant . . . as foolish, incorrect, and just as incorrect whether one supposes history has a goal in socialism, or progress, or any political *ism*. I am ambivalent in my idea of history, or the history of ideas, as I am ambivalent towards the above in any human nature. There are no sure political aims inherent in human nature, while there may be sure vices that favour some forms of societal organisation more than others, and there is *no automatic selection* (of political ideas and regimes) *which conforms with our moral requirements.*

Concepts such as reason, progress, or the basic adherence to facts and truth, are theoretical possibilities, and we are ill-equipped in their application to prevent tragedy or otherwise ensure moral or technical progress. They are not intrinsic, they won't be automatically or organically victorious, and despite various sophisticated objections many still believe, emotionally, in a universe bent towards justice or progress. Some liberals suggest humans are inherently rational, presenting an idealistic concept of human motives that remains abstract and easily eroded. One can't be naively optimistic about human vices. Ideologies need to contend with people being irrational or emotional. La Rochefoucauld should remind us: we often lack the strength to follow reason fully, and we are tremendously unreasonable. Ignorance, or stupidity, very much play a role in history and political action. I cannot say progress is impossible, I do not, and I certainly do want progressions in justice and equity. Yet it is still the case given human freedom or the unpredictability of future existence that we cannot say progress is obvious, natural, or probable; and I'm prone to being pessimistic. A truer philosophy of history allows us fewer settled convictions.

Many sorts of liberals, neoliberals, anarchists of various stripes, communists, conservatives, free market libertarians, popular right-wing insurrectionists, and fascists reject the above in some way—they can be inclined to a belief in their own existential superiority and the certain, even axiomatic quality of their plans. They can be too confident in their justifications of themselves and in their understanding of their opponents. Of course some may be more modest, or truthful, and not believe that their ideas are so clearly justified, whatever they are—but I'd contend that many still suppose their view of reality, their philosophy, their ideology, is obvious, *common sense*, or evidently true—and that it should be obvious to others. This entails a few things, I think: a mistaken assumption on the workings of history, the scope of human rationality, the inept conveyance of perceived better ideas, a sense of what is contingent, and a false sense of how one's own ideas (or antagonistic ideas) proliferate or are soon rejected. I can think I have good ideas, or maybe know what's in our better interest (or at least mine), but this does not mean my views are popular, self-evident, achievable, and that common incentives mean things I'm opposed to don't have an easier time getting their way. I don't suppose humans are inherently good either; we are more likely to gratify our passions, and it requires an exhaustingly difficult process to incentivise better behaviour without resulting in tyranny or anarchy.

". . . the liberal believes in the permanence of humanity's imperfection, he resigns himself to a regime in which the good will be the result of numberless actions, and never the object of a conscious choice. Finally, he subscribes to the pessimism that sees, in politics, the art of creating the conditions in which the vices of men will contribute to the good of the state."—Raymond Aron, *The Opium of The Intellectuals.*

This is opposed to a sometimes-liberal conceit that moral persuasion and an inherent goodness in humanity can promote a broadly humanistic, rational and free society. I suppose that some varieties of progress and justice are genuine, and I reasonably do not disagree with righteous diagnoses of our moral and societal failures. The ideas and applications of progress, freedom, justice, equality are all a grinding affair, a difficult marathon, easily ruined, readily degraded,

while a mediocre performance being the least bad possibility is immediately aesthetically unpopular today just as it was in the 1950s or around the publication of Aron's *Introduction à la philosophie de l'histoire*, or in antiquity. We may resonate more with impatient demands. Technological progress reveals greater moral failures, as moral justice does not follow so soon from industrial prosperity. We are rightly disillusioned and justly not content with our lot, with continued abuse, with a type of hopeless resignation to injustice and a slow crawl that may quickly be halted or reversed. We demand more and it's no doubt good to dream of better futures. These are noble wishes.

What's still eternally of concern is what John Milton called "the known rules of ancient liberty". This does not mean we are resigned to a slow and hollow Burkeanism. The socialist Proudhon, the liberal Tocqueville, and Karl Marx were all severe in their criticisms of the *imitators* of the Great Revolution, 'the comedians of 1848'. Mary Wollstonecraft, whose ideas we take for granted, knew the dangers of revolt much like others. The fight for liberty doesn't presume morality or good politics. To use another famous expression, it's one of the easiest and most regrettable processes for revolt and revolution, in the name of good causes or not, to be hoisted by its own petard. Pessimism becomes more reasonable, while we are hopefully not resigned to it. Strategy and good tactics are alien concepts to many revolutionaries. What miraculous formula is there that could rid us of our inequalities? This isn't some cheap question. It's easy for some

honestly answer, but this doesn't suppose in-
telligible, let alone politicised, ways of achieving
. I'm sorry for being doubtful; I'd much rather
have fewer doubts and it's still much worth it, af-
ter all this caution, for people to optimistically
dream.

## Conclusion

While I am not bold enough to suggest what will
surely work—equivocation is sort of the point—
this doesn't suppose anyone else, even if guilty of
their own failures, can't analyse vital flaws in
others.

With all this I've likely failed to give a distilled,
clearer definition of a better societal organisa-
tion; nor, probably, have I cleared up the confu-
sion around the multiplicity of definitions for
liberalism. I've mostly made negative sugges-
tions against a type of historicism or teleological
ideology that is not unique to varieties of liberal-
ism, with the vague hope against the odds that
others might do better. We do better if we know
the fragility of espoused ideological principles,
and we do better if we know the confusing dif-
ferences between ideas and their practice, and
yet . . . If equivocation is an intellectual strength
in some regard, then it's easily a practical weak-
ness in others. How is an idea that's inherently
equivocal supposed to succeed? I doubt the
equivocating and pluralistic ideas I align with,
or share with the likes of Aron, will have an easy
time finding a good application to modern soci-
ety or finding much influence. I can rightly cri-
tique the wrongdoing of any sort of doctrinaire
ideology, but that doesn't mean such critiques
will lead to (physical) success—even if they are
more astute, more sophisticated, and more
aware of the failures of past regimes. I'm bad at
pretending to be a scholar and it's easy for me to
cheap-out and direct a reader to others with far
more depth, breadth, and precision in their
analysis. Laziness doesn't help either. I at least

hope that I have hinted at an importance in dif-
ferent meanings, a keener (while imperfect)
awareness of philosophical underpinnings, and
it's still a good affirmation to note the foolish-
ness and dishonesty of overly-teleological ideas.

Liberalism, in its better iterations, is constitu-
tively pluralistic and conscious of history; and
so, if we want to be more truthful and consistent,
this requires less dogmatism and more fluidity—
which is both positive and negative. It's much
more difficult, I think, to have a settled ortho-
doxy that is 'liberal' than a settled orthodoxy
that is not: it is more constitutively vulnerable
than other influences. A clear orthodoxy is often
regarded as helpful, but as I hope I have de-
tailed, an apparently righteous historicism, be it
socialist, liberal, capitalist, conservative, or oth-
erwise, can predictably lead to demagoguery,
crimes, and failure. Caution, prudence or wari-
ness about optimistic and utopian aims mean we
may be less likely to produce prejudicial results—
although what negatives we tolerate or the ca-
pacity to remain in power is another matter.

Political ideas of the same name can prove
vastly different depending on prior psychology,
persuasive limits, humility, or one's epistemol-
ogy of history. If one wants a better understand-
ing of politics, then it helps to navigate the diver-
sity of meanings, even if one rejects my analysis
of liberal thought—especially given, as I'll always
admit, the easily perceptible failures and
hypocrisy of modern liberal regimes. People
should not, I hope, become too comfortable and
confident in what they perceive as possible. The
dim dream of a better world requires diligence
and prudence just as much as it may require
courage and impatience, lest so much effort re-
sult in ruin.

I doubt the above is very persuasive. The best
result would be to accept something of what I've
said here—though I'm mostly a conduit for oth-
ers—and then prove me wrong.

Thomas Walton

# Unsavory Thoughts

## Who's Will Oldham?

It seems like one of those things people say, that there are only six archetypal characters, and we more or less all fall into them. In some way.

I once knew someone, a friend but not a close friend, more than an acquaintance, though, but less than an intimate, yet definitely more than a friend of a friend . . . Anyway, he was someone I knew and had drinks with on occasion, and he seemed to fall pretty clearly into one of the six archetypes. His wife did anyway. If you marry an archetypal character, surely that makes you one too, right? I guess I'm not sure.

This friend and I used to live in the same neighborhood in LA. He married a woman in the film industry. She was mostly an actor. By her own account she was a great actor. By all accounts she was beautiful. The only people who thought she wasn't beautiful were people who resented her beauty. To these people she was pretentious. I never saw her act. Not on screen anyway.

My friend was overjoyed that she agreed to marry him. Their seduction was quick, and a bit lopsided. He was head over heels in love with her, and she knew it. With a blasé flip of her wrist, she agreed to tolerate him in marriage. I should mention that he was not ugly. In fact, he was very handsome, and people said so. That's why she agreed to marry him. She wanted beautiful children and together they would certainly make them.

I lost track of them when they moved from LA to his parents' small town. Nearly twenty years passed. I didn't really think of them that much. He wasn't a close friend.

Then, weirdly, we found ourselves living in St. Louis. All of us. My wife and child. And the two of them and their kids (all beautiful). My wife's aunt lived in St. Louis. She was having some health issues, so we moved there to help out. wasn't terrible. It was fine. I loved the way the summer nights stayed warm and humid. In St Louis, you can sweat sitting still.

We started hanging out again. My friend and They had a little backyard, and we would go over for barbecues. She floated across the patio as she were starring in a film from the Criterio Collection, with her creme de violette and he martini glass. There was an enormous oak tree off the patio. The grass beneath it wouldn't grow It was always dark, and always damp. The su just couldn't break through. In the winter th acorns were everywhere. You could hardly wall But in the summer, at the backyard barbecue: my friend's wife's air of elegance bedazzled th scene. It was as if we were in the Hollywoo Hills, and not The Delmar Loop.

I could see there was something else there now, too. She was in her forties, still lovely, bu unable to hide the fact she resented her positio in life. She always spoke of the people sh worked with in LA, in her 20s. Some of them ha gotten somewhat famous, and she dropped thei names in a weird display of what might hav been. He worked in a minor role at an indepen dent radio station, and she would mentio meeting this or that musician. We were sup posed to be impressed. We rarely were—Who' Will Oldham?—but we would politely lift ou eyebrows as if to say, "wow, you met *him* . . ."

She didn't work. She hadn't acted in years One of the kids had behavioral issues. They hac to take him out of school. She was homeschool ing him. The marriage was struggling. Sh blamed my friend for her misery and spoke openly about how he had no ambition.

It was difficult for us to witness. She said once drunk on champagne, that she married the wrong man. She should've married someone ir film. A director. Someone with drive or money o both. She should've stayed in LA. She said this out loud! There, on the patio under the oak tree Beautiful kids falling out of her, clinging to her After she said it, she laughed and said, "oh well . . . cheers!" She raised her glass and we al awkwardly raised ours, even her husband, in a toast to what exactly, I'm not sure.

This went on for a few years. Those depressing backyard barbecues. We spent a Thanksgiving with them, once. And New Year's. Despite the tragedy of the situation, I liked them. I liked him a lot. I started to think of him as a close friend, much more than an acquaintance, something close to an intimate, certainly more than a friend of a friend.

Then we moved back to the coast. It's been a few years. I've lost touch with him again. The kids would be teenagers by now, nearly out of the house, but at least one or two of them would still be in the house. I have no idea if they're still together, still in St. Louis, if she's still floating across that patio beneath that enormous tree. It's weird, sometimes I think of them. There in the backyard, drunk. Just sitting there not talking to each other. He staring at her, and she holding a martini glass with a distant look in her eye. Acorns everywhere on the ground.

## At the Giacometti Exhibit

We were at the Giacometti exhibit. The crowds were thick. It wasn't easy to be alone with the sculptures. *Walking Man* was absolutely thronged. And so was *Standing Woman*. The fact that so many people wanted to see these two enormous sculptures made me like them less. Both the sculptures and the people. I'm sure that's a petty response on my part, but that's the one I had.

I spent most of my time staring into a long glass case. Inside was a forest of miniature sculptures. All of them just as profound as the large ones, *Walking Man* and *Standing Woman*. More so, for me. They were restrained, unobtrusive, they didn't walk right out in front of you but hid in obscurity, doing their own thing, nothing really. Just going on having been made by Giacometti's hands over 70 years ago.

Near the case a man in a black hoodie, beard and ill-fitting pants, started laughing uncontrollably. The other museum goers seemed to be afraid of him. Was he homeless? Mentally ill? On drugs? Everyone was avoiding him. I heard someone say they were going to get security.

"What is it?" I asked the laughing man.

"Look," he said, and pointed at a tiny sculpture of a figure, only an inch or two high.

"I see," I said, "I guess it *is* sort of funny in a way."

"No," he said, "look at the whole thing."

And then I realized what the laughing man was laughing at. At least I think I did. Beneath the tiny figure was an enormous plinth that Giacometti had also cast in bronze. That is, it was part of the sculpture. The whole thing—plinth and figure—were cast as one contiguous (massive) block of bronze. The tiny man was a fraction of the work, not merely sitting on an enormous plinth. So that most of the sculpture, nearly all of it, was the thing that the tiny man was standing on. Because of the enormity of the plinth and the so-small-as-to-nearly-not-exist-at-all size of the figure, there was a sense of extreme isolation and loneliness.

"I see," I said.

"Yes," the laughing man said.

"That's good," I said.

"Good," the laughing man laughed again, "it's hilarious!"

I stared for a few minutes longer, and then I too started laughing. The laughing man and I stood there, looking at the enormous plinth and the tiny man. We were both laughing now, laughing together, *Two Laughing Men*, when *Three Security Guards* came and asked us both to leave.

I said something feeble like, "but my wife is here. . ." But the *Three Security Guards* were unmoved. Bored as bronze sculptures, they gestured blandly toward the door.

Qianqian Liu

# The Wrk

Recently I learnt the correct way to use **parentheses** when two **parentheticals** [*baby kangaroo*] are presented is to create a [*pocket*] so if I have five parentheticals [*a kangaroo family*] I will use |n{u(g[g]e)t}s|; I can also add a door ⌐o⌐ to keep kangaroos from disrupting chickens.

```
Oftentimes I get carried away
tomushtosooth
Soredough
mishemishehumptyhead
nomnom
Ulmunn
shleepy
dahth
shleepydahth
by parenthetical thoughts and go elsewhere.
Not today.
```

A parergon is anything that could go into my refraigerator (physically and metaphysically) that's not my *friodge* and the floor it stands on. A refrigerator does not openly exhibit its parergonality. You need to stare the hell out of the refrigerator to see the **abyss**[1]. The **way** to each other's philosophy or *dao* is to describe our refrigerators to each other. We'd understand a lot of good & evil, up & down, left & right relationally by faithfully describing our refrigerators—I would describe mine in great detail so you get a unity of parerga, and you would describe yours to me and I'd ask questions about your refrigerator, through which I'd identify the pleasing object, the beautiful, or simply have an aesthetic affection with the presentness of your description.

|,| this is a mini *friodge* to keep apple juice

How often do you open your refrigerator just to watch the light turn on? How long do you keep leftovers or do you throw food away? How many brands of bagels do you stockpile? Do you store 1st edition old books in the freezer? Do you believe your refrigerator is a portal to parallel worlds or possibly a cat island and most importantly! A cinnamon raisin bagel is theoretically a dessert, therefore a cinnamon raisin bagel is a donut. Am I a food-tyrant if I insist a cinnamon raisin bagel which contains 11 grams of sugar (Dave's Killer brand) is tautologically the same as a donut? When I say boiled sourdough tastes wonderful, am I exoticizing the act of boiling sour doughs?

My old *freoidge* in Beijing was partially burnt and with no shelves, bags and containers piled onto each other at a slant like Sisyphus' job site. My dad could always locate the bag of food he wanted to cook in the apocalyptic landscape of the *freoidge*. What kind of landscape does your fridge have? Does it look like a fairyland? Does it have a lakeview? Is it deserted? Is it gentrified? Do you put up magnets and your sense of pride on the fridge door

to awe visitors? Is your fridge lonely? After you take a step back from your

fridge, can you tell whether a person is in a toxic relationship by observing

the level of food deterioration in the refrigerator? Do you completely clear out your refrigerator and unplug it when you need to spend a couple of weeks to take time out or do you leave some food behind so there will be food when you come back? Do you think deep thoughts or plot revenges when rearranging yogurts by their expiration dates? All of these questions are parergonal to the question of "what's the meaning of life?", "what's wrong with you?", and "what is arrhaat?". Posthooman life is filled with parergonal problems that come into being, become aware of itself or reveal itself through a lack (a vibration, a vacillation) and we diligently supplement this lack without ever filling it and without indulging in multiples [when a freezer is stuffed with doughs, it roars. Rawr! (I think freeza sounds better? free-zah! It sounds like a mantra that turns on lights in all the refrigerators across the globe)] because according to Lacan the essence of our ego is nothing but frustration; this incompleteness is either detachable or ill-detachable[2] from the ego (or whatever intricacies

---

[1] *what we are looking for is not the truth of essence but rather the essence of truth. A curious entanglement reveals itself... Is it a mere curiosity, is it the vacuous hair-splitting of a playing with concepts, or is it an abyss*, The Origin of the Work of Art, *Page 27*

[2] *The question of desire, of pleasure and displeasure, is also that of a detachment.* The Truth of Painting. *Page 39*

ve have), the point is, we place ourselves in the place of others (see this? a parerga for a parerga. I just took a break and read something interesting, check this out: "the anal drive has a lot to do with shit so we can replace the verb gaze with the verb shit, we can say that the subject shits out an object, or is shited out. Obsessive neurotics feel that they are being shit out all the time. The Other rejects the subject like a shit. You need to eat, you need to shit, you don't apparently need the Other's gaze or voice, but you nevertheless desire it more than you know.[1]" The other day I was advised not to disperse readers with parenthetical sparks so let's continue the pre-parenthetical thoughts) in order to enjoy/suffer, so the point is, the intrinsic beauty of my *refyragerater* is beyond itself, but it is also delimited in a particular way that this refyragerater is the ground for all our meditations on the parergonality of refrigerators. My *refradgrator* solves problems and resolves disharmonies. Everybody has their own case with refrigerators, my *refradgerator* is a reflection of my death drive (yay to fat and carbohydrates!). Parergon is jouissance (I couldn't spell the word Washignton at my citizenship test but I correctly spelt Jouissance all the time. I failed the test because I gave three different wrong answers to "who is your house of representative?" It somehow brings me joy to think about how I failed the test. I didn't know I couldn't spell the word Whashignton till that particular day) for parergon is superfluous or insufficient (*ergon*- pleasure, *parergon*- beyond pleasure).

[— —] this is a large freezer to hide the bodies of loved ones

> I'll be eating lightly boiled fish and shrimp
> over rice over a tortilla in a dish that doesn't
> fit the 6inch free space on my desk in front
> of my laptop stacked on top of a stack of old
> books and whenever I eat noodles it spills onto
> the laptop and the book spines so I always cover the keyboard and books with a thick towel so
> I can watch tv shows on my laptop while eating
> noodles. I wish I had a proper tv so my wall
> has something it can frame to.

---

[1] Reading Seminar XI—*Lacan's* Four fundamental concepts of psychoanalysis. *Page 143*

KURT LUCHS

# HERE WE COME A-LEWIS CARROLLING

## OR, SOME SENSIBLE THOUGHTS ON THE NONSENSE OF "JABBERWOCKY"

What is the most famous nonsense poem in the English language? If you guessed "The Wasteland" by T. S. Eliot, or "Leaving the Atocha Station" by John Ashbery, or "oxygen" by Aram Saroyan, or any of various mid-20th century American billboards featuring Burma Shave, you'd be close but no cigar. The hands-down winner, as declared unanimously by the judges (me and history), is "Jabberwocky" by Lewis Carroll, aka Charles Dodgson (1832–1898).

The poem first appeared in 1871 in *Through the Looking-Glass, and What Alice Found There*, the sequel to *Alice's Adventures in Wonderland*. Those two books and the mock-epic poem *The Hunting of the Snark* constitute the entire basis of Carroll's literary reputation, and they are more than enough. "Jabberwocky" is a highlight of *Through the Looking-Glass* and has come to have a life of its own, inspiring any number of tributes, imitations and references in the century and a half since it first greeted the world. To wit:

In 1968 a British studio group released a silly psychedelic pop single called "Jabberwock," backed with "Which Dreamed It." Both songs were adapted from Carroll poems, as was the group's name, Boeing Duveen and the Beautiful Soup. The leader was Sam Hutt, in real life a physician and friend of Pink Floyd, and the record was produced by a young Tony Visconti, before he became David Bowie's frequent collaborator. You can find the songs on YouTube or in the second box of the *Rubble* collection.

Donovan wrote his own musical backing for "Jabberwocky" and released it on one of his least-known albums, *HMS Donovan* (1971). This double-LP collection of children's songs also includes a version of Carroll's "The Walrus and the

Carpenter" and "The Owl and the Pussycat" by Carroll's main competitor in the nonsense verse sweepstakes, Edward Lear. Of course, given today's declining educational standards, these song-poems are over the heads of most adults, let alone children.

Saturday Night Live was still in its first season on February 21, 1976, when Desi Arnaz hosted Episode 14. He proved to be quite good at it. There are many great moments, such as his performance of the songs "Cuban Pete" and "Babalu" with son Desi Arnaz, Jr. (late of Dino, Desi and Billy). But the best sequence is when he recites "Jabberwocky" in that cockeyed Cuban accent of his, seeming to improvise his own jokes and comments. There is something very moving about seeing this 19th century classic lovingly manhandled by one of the comedic icons of 1950s television as he passes the torch to the Not Ready for Primetime Players, who would determine the course of comedy for the next few decades, and even now.

The following year, Terry Gilliam made his solo directorial debut with *Jabberwocky*, a rambunctious if uneven film that appeared to want to carry on where *Monty Python and the Holy Grail* had left off. Only loosely based on the Carroll poem, it featured Gilliam, Terry Jones and "Seventh Python" Neil Innes in smaller roles, with Michael Palin in the lead. While it probably did not cause Carroll to spin in his grave, neither was it likely to help him sleep the big sleep more peacefully.

I could go on. I could tell you what *The Muppet Show* did with the poem in 1980 (very clever actually), but you get the point. "Jabberwocky" is here to stay. It has woven itself into our culture, high and low. I haven't even mentioned its effect on other writers, such as James Joyce. We might as well get on with appreciating why it keeps resonating with us in so many ways.

Carroll began the poem in 1855, finishing the first stanza and sharing it with his family. Even in this larval form it is a powerful bit of fun:

'Twas brillig, and the slithy toves
    Did gyre and gimble in the wabe:
All mimsy were the borogoves,
    And the mome raths outgrabe.

The first thing one notices is the abundance of nonce words, invented words. By my count there are ten of them in this stanza alone. As Alice says after reading the whole poem, "Somehow it seems to fill my head with ideas—only I don't know exactly what they are!" And that is what the author intended, intentional fallacy be damned. Though we can't know precisely what is happening, it is somewhat ominous and dreadful, partly, perhaps, for that very reason. Those "slithy toves" sound perfectly awful, and I have no wish to see them "gimble in the wabe." I have no idea what the "mome raths" are, but I'm pretty sure I don't ever want them to "outgrabe" me.

This first stanza contains the most notable use of the word "gyre" in English verse until Yeats resurrected it for his own "The Second Coming." Come to think of it, his "rough beast . . . slouching towards Bethlehem to be born" owes more than a little to the Jabberwock. Both poems play on our dread, one for humor, the other for horror.

Back to you, Mr. Carroll! At this early stage he titled the fragment "Stanza of Anglo-Saxon Poetry." It does indeed sound medieval. One scholar also heard echoes of Shakespeare in it, specifically a passage in Act I Scene 1 of *Hamlet* where "the sheeted dead / Did squeak and gibber in the Roman streets." However, I don't mean to go down the rabbit hole with Alice and get lost in all of the possible sources of the poem. The point is, whatever odds and ends were rattling around in Carroll's well-read head, this is what came out. As with any poem worth reading, it must stand on its own two scaly feet. On to stanza two:

"Beware the Jabberwock, my son!
    The jaws that bite, the claws that catch!
Beware the Jubjub bird, and shun
    The frumious Bandersnatch!"

Remember when I promised to stop bringing up pop culture references to the poem? Well, I lied. I have to mention that Frumious Bandersnatch was the name of a Berkeley-based sixties psychedelic group whose members would later become part of the Steve Miller Band and Journey.

By the way, who is speaking in this stanza? He calls our unnamed hero "son," but is he really his father? Or perhaps his father confessor? Priests often do have prominent roles in medieval literature. Unfortunately, without a DNA test we'll never know.

Regardless, this stanza serves to introduce the titular monster. And, though we haven't mentioned the actual poetry of the poem yet, there is quite a bit of it in these first two stanzas. They are composed of quatrains with an ABAB rhyme scheme and an iambic meter. There are generally eight syllables per line, except for the last line, which has six (the end line of stanza two has seven syllables, making it the lone exception in the poem). We have alliteration aplenty: "gyre and gimble"; "mimsy" and "mome"; "Jabberwock," "jaws," "Jubjub"; "claws" and "catch". I could only locate one clear instance of assonance: "Jubjub" and "shun".

Stanza three finds our anonymous protagonist about to engage the beast, only he suddenly decides to pull a Hamlet:

> He took his vorpal blade in hand;
>   Longtime the manxsome foe he sought—
> So rested he by the Tumtum tree
>   And stood awhile in thought.

After all, it's only a Jabberwock on the loose. We can afford to take a little rest break by the Tumtum tree, yes? Another thing to notice here is the departure from the rhyme scheme we started with. This stanza is ABCB. Further, because C doesn't rhyme with A, Carroll gives it an internal rhyme with "he" and "tree".

Now we get to the main action in stanzas four and five:

s

> And, as in uffish thought he stood,
>   The Jabberwock, with eyes of flame,
> Came whiffling through the tulgey wood,
>   And burbled as it came!

> One, two! One, two! And through and through
>   The vorpal blade went snicker-snack!
> He left it dead, and with its head
>   He went galumphing back.

Stanza four returns to the original rhyme scheme of ABAB. Stanza five uses the ABCB scheme of stanza three, with another internal rhyme in C, "dead" and "head". "Uffish" certainly sounds like a close relative of "oafish". "Eyes of flame" strongly suggests that we are dealing with some sort of dragon. As for the last line of stanza four, I have known several creatures who burbled as they came, but this is a family magazine. "Galumphing" is one of several nonce words coined for the poem that have since become neologisms, that is to say, words fully accepted into the language, with their own dictionary entries and everything. At any rate, despite his dawdling and diffidence our hero has managed to kill and decapitate the Jabberwock. And in the penultimate stanza, number six, he receives a hero's welcome:

> "And hast thou slain the Jabberwock?
>   Come to my arms, my beamish boy!
> O frabjous day! Callooh! Callay!"
>   He chortled in his joy.

Again he employs the ABCB rhyme scheme with an internal rhyme in C. The last line gives us another nonce word, "chortled," that has become a neologism. In fact, I use it in one of my two tribute poems to "Jabberwocky" below. Carroll may have thought he was coining the word "beamish," though it has its own obscure, respectable lineage. There is no question that he coined "frabjous" and "callooh" and "callay," which are wonderful words. If we all keep using them, they too will enter the language as this poem has entered our culture.

Carroll could have easily ended the poem there. Instead, he repeats stanza one, making the poem into a circular journey, what in his time might have been described as a Sisyphean struggle, or in ours as a time loop. The implication is that there is always another Jabberwock, or a Jubjub bird, or a frumious Bandersnatch, just as in *Buffy the Vampire Slayer* there is always another apocalypse.

As is the way of most classics, "Jabberwocky" has influenced generations of writers of all types. I mentioned Joyce and Yeats. I would also say that authors as diverse as Jorge Luis Borges,

Kurt Vonnegut, P. G. Wodehouse, Gertrude Stein, Thomas Pynchon and the whole New York School of Poets have taken much of value from Lewis Carroll, aside from the pure pleasure his work offers.

At the beginning of this essay I made light of what I consider a completely impenetrable poem by John Ashbery, "Leaving the Atocha Station," from what some readers would agree is his most difficult, confounding book, *The Tennis Court Oath*. Yet with a slightly less extreme application of the same techniques, learned in part from "nonsense" poems such as "Jabberwocky," Ashbery and his compatriots created some masterpieces too. And that is one more reason to be grateful to Mr. Carroll for bringing forth his burbling beast.

# A Nonsense Verse

*(Unfortunately, Not Written by Lewis Carroll or Edward Lear)*

When men were men, and women were men,
And the rest of us were trying to rest,
They picked a number from one to ten
But which they picked is anyone's guess.

For on a spinning top there stands
A man whose face could use a rinse,
And coiling slyly in his hands
Are miles and miles of finger prints.

Yet there is hope for those who sneeze
And those who drive the Shriner's car:
If half the locks fit half the keys
Then maybe the jam will fit the jar.

# A Literary Limerick

A gentleman named T. S. Eliot
Is heaven's wittiest man of belles lettres.
"I think I'm immortal,"
He says with a chortle,
"But God knows it's too early to tell yet."

Israel Bonilla

# Remnant

Yakov has a peculiar way of worrying, eyes always set on immortality. He walks as if hunched by the weight of yet-to-be-born thousands, who all have a claim to some part of his being. He speaks as if hesitance were to ruin a potential aphorism, believing his colleagues variants of Boswell. And, of course, he is cautious not to bring too much attention upon himself; long ago he must have resolved that to play the dandy would be unbecoming of someone as plain-featured as he. But has it been wise to play the misanthrope, to sigh at the view of a living world?

I caught a glimpse of his green checkered shirt at one of Karla's gatherings. Most of the attendees had an academic connection to philosophy, so it is easy to imagine the atmosphere: no gravitas, only irreverence. It was an act of unusual boldness to maintain a scowl amid the grins. And there he was, atypical, gripping his cup of anything but wine, exchanging the occasional word with Karla, who took her time before presenting us.

"So you do care once in a while, sæti. Look, here's your match."

"It's nothing personal. I like to work at night. What can one do?"

"This is a habit of his, Yakovlevich. Silva is rude that way."

"Pay no attention. You must know her by now."

"Silva. Like the poet?"

"You like literature?"

"Ha! That is an understatement."

"I do, yes."

"Refreshing. One hears about it only in journals. Mainly as a way to illustrate some obscure philosophical point."

"Is that right? I guess you enjoy it, then."

"There's a caveat: when I have the time."

"Oh, Silva, always the gentleman. It's nice to see both of you share some common ground. I will be leaving. I'm positive I've heard whatever is to follow."

I expected Karla's quirky jab to lighten the mood, but Yakov did not budge. His seriousness, however, contrasted with his voice, which grew high-pitched as we delved deeper into other subjects.

"I would rather live like your namesake, yes."

"Now I see what captured Karla's imagination."

"What do you mean?"

"She gets bored of the chatter. Have you had a chance to speak with someone other than her?"

"No."

"Great. You would be bombarded with Socratic irony. 'Ah, *intensity*, that is a rather opaque term. Do we not *also* use it to describe *trifles*? Please do *tell* how is it that its use in poetry differs.' And so on. They don't really care. At least not in my experience. What matters is showing that you're as confused as any bumbling idiot."

"I am familiar with the type. I studied philosophy years ago."

"That seems to me an important detail. Why didn't you mention it?"

"I gave it up after a while. It is a trivial part of my life. Nothing good came of it."

"And here you are, speaking with a specialist in Dewey's philosophy of mind."

Yakov's faux-deep voice crept back and not much else was said.

Even if our conversation was too casual then, there were details that in hindsight appear significant: the deliberate pause between each sentence, the subtle nudge toward time-honored obsessions, the fluctuations of tone, the adamantine scowl. I liked him despite the I-would-rathers.

We saw each other only at Karla's gatherings, which meant that any possibility of friendship was low. He always sat in the same corner, near the same chair. And Karla was always hovering by. She talked with him for long intervals, offered him drinks and underlined books. I had imagined he was laconic with her, but no. Were her displays of affection maternal, fraternal or romantic? Hard to say. As soon as I went for maternal, she played with his hair; for romantic, she annoyed him with some practical joke; for fraternal, she rubbed his shoulder while gazing at him with condescending eyes. In all instances, he seemed uncomfortable. Suddenly, I had before me another telling detail, or rather an explanation. His seriousness was not organic. It was a way of dealing with his body. I believed my conjectures to be sound.

"But these intellectual types are always a bit awkward, right? Look around."

"They are no more awkward than anyone at any party. Aside from the extroversion machines that make a point of their presence, of course."

"You mean that? Both of us are living proof of those *not very comfortable in their skin*."

"I disagree."

"If there are extroversion machines, surely there are introversion machines."

"Yes, and there are none here."

"Okay, I'll be blunter. Laughing is a sign of being socially at ease. How often do you laugh?"

"I understand. Your example was not inadvertent."

"This is not personal. Really, it isn't."

"If you have to know, I find humor in simple things. People falling, for example. Otherwise, it feels contrived."

I could not take these words at face value; he was patently irritated. But they left me more curious. Here was an educated man defending his dignity by appealing to slapstick.

Karla thought little of my speculations. She gave him greater leeway than I did. The roulette kept spinning—maternal, fraternal, romantic.

"I've known him for years. You've just known him for months. So I have the upper hand."

"How unphilosophical, K. You're actually at a disadvantage. You're too close. You are more familiar with the way he wants to portray himself. I have a clearer view."

"Silly, silly Silva. What do you know about him? Go ahead, tell me."

"Let's see. He says he loves literature, poetry specifically. I think that has more to do with trying to distance himself from *professors of philosophy*. He says he also loves philosophy, analytical specifically. Easy: he doesn't want to be classed with soft-minded *littérateurs*. He says he cares little for worldly success. Easier: he wants to distance himself from *us*."

"Very articulate handling of stereotypes. But I'm sorry to say that Yakovlevich is absent."

"Is he? Illuminate me, then."

"You see, something important is missing. He's a person, not an abstraction. But you can't find this obviously true. The fact that you don't know a thing about his life messes with your attempts at explanation. And this applies to all you've said about his seriousness too."

"That's why you're struggling for tenure."

"Oh, Silva, what would I do without your idiotic jokes?"

"Believe I'm not unlike the Yakovs of the world."

"You're a person, Silva, no doubt about that."

Karla did emphasize a partial truth. I knew almost nothing of Yakov's life. This was a subject toward which his nudges never pointed. He had studied philosophy once and wrote poetry (and perhaps some philosophy). Yet life isn't just a series of exercises for memory; it also comprises our day-to-day thoughts and foibles. Our conversations were part of his life, make-believe and everything. Though slight, I had a hold of Yakov.

Predictably, Karla got tired of the crowded evenings. She moved out to a smaller place and rescaled the old routine. Twice a month Yakov, Irene, Thomas, and I went over. Irene and Thomas were an obvious choice. Thomas was a close friend of Karla's in high school. He became an entrepreneur (therapy on demand, test preparation, café, used bookstore). Irene, whom he married, studied law and helped out early on. Their cosmopolitan sensibilities worked perfectly to check everybody's provincial attitudes but Yakov's. And in this more intimate atmosphere I grasped what was missing.

"Where's the lure of posterity? I suspect it always follows a pattern of disappointment. In an arid life it must be a comforting mirage."

"A mirage? Just look at us, continuing the genuflection to heroes."

"Right. But they will never taste this posthumous glory. The present you *can* taste."

"I take it, Thomas, that you're making a case for your life."

"No. I'm not in the business of justifying my zest."

"Any thoughts, Yakovlevich?"

"I disagree. The scope of the present is poor. One can reach out to few. Casting your work into the future guarantees sympathetic ears, however disagreeable."

"Does that matter other than in an abstract way? It is a tortuous route toward pleasure."

"It is vaguely related to pleasure. I would rather believe it has to do with multiplying one's possibilities. Here, I can be a modest number of Yakov's: Silva´s, Karla´s, Thomas's, Irene's. There, I will be boundless."

"Which is pleasurable."

"No. It is a metaphysical thirst. I resist tying it to something as homely as pleasure."

"You see, this is the type of discourse I find baffling. It's relentlessly abstract. Life is left aside."

"Life. That word's connotations are baffling—sense stimulation, excess, haste."

"Energy. That is it."

Those were the usual disagreements between Thomas and Yakov. And so long as I didn't intervene, Yakov remained polite. He knew I pursued questions of theory until they collapsed into psychology. His psychology. This subject, posterity, proved important. There was the center I sought. So I led Thomas and waited for their discussions. Thomas shared the way in which I approached reality. Both of us lived oblivious to a future judgment. We had no invisible beads hanging from our necks.

Yakov's religious upbringing became steadily visible. His father insisted on God's watchfulness. Soon Yakov felt the inhibition of his will. All acts and thoughts had an audience. What's more: a discriminating and uptight audience. If he swore, his impious words were heard through the chambers of heaven. If he bore ill-will, the heat of his heart enraged the overseer. The prison formed in childhood is a perennial prison.

The novelty of Yakov ceased, and Thomas had no interest left for more facts of life. Irene, owing to her politeness, was the only one who asked about this or that biographical detail.

The gatherings also came to an abrupt end when Yakov was hired as a teacher of poetry in some nameless high school thirty minutes east of Palm Springs. Now he was in the habit of inviting us to visit separately. It was in one of these visits that I felt compelled to inquire at length about his ways.

We met at a charming little park, unlike most you find in California. There were no traces of Park Advisory Council regulations, just an entanglement of wooden benches, rustic seesaws, and bull thistle. There, Yakov sat on a trunk, a navy blue rundown briefcase at his side. He was drinking from a thermos.

"How long have we known each other?"

"Three, four years? I don't count."

"Strange. This has been something of an impersonal friendship."

"Always from your end."

"I . . ."

"Disagree? I'd imagine."

"Your eyes are too open. I feel myself a case study in your presence."

"You seem to wish for that treatment. I'm sure you're self-aware."

"We all are when we understand that others also devote their time to remembrance."

"In a bookish sense, Yakov."

"I forget. You and Thomas, ever the lovers of clear-cut distinctions."

"You've been in touch with him?"

"No. I wish him well, though."

"Anyway, bookish, deliberate. I never bought your idea of possibilities."

"I was not selling, clearly."

"You are unambiguous."

"That would be foolish of me, wouldn't it? I'm not that coarse. But I've been meaning to make a concession to you."

"I'm here."

"I do have a pronounced sense of discomfort. It has followed me around most of my life. That is all I can concede. I don't understand its nature. Your conjectures are as good as any."

"There's a lot to work with."

"Unfortunately, I am skeptical about the uses of autobiography. Right here, talking with you, I have a guess. I am too in love with the past in which I had no business existing. The past of the poets, of the novelists, of the philosophers. Yes. I am not concerned with the undeveloped present, with the would-be monuments. Yes. But let us stop. This is all there is to it. An old-school egoist."

With a mystifying nod he settled the matter. We had a pleasant afternoon, perhaps the very first one that I enjoyed in his company. And more would follow.

So, Yakov, are you wise? Only if the real lies elsewhere.

Jake La Botz

# Sponsors

Don Goodrich cleans and shaves the body of his current tenant while the oldies station, KQRS, hums in the background. He begins replacing blood, bile, and urine with embalming solution just as the 12-string guitar intro to The Eagles' *Hotel California* comes weeping out of his wall-mounted speakers. The oft-repeated recording—itself embalmed and immortalized, spinning incessantly from a DJ-less digital hub somewhere in space—is comforting to Don as it is to the millions of other classic rock connoisseurs who know every verse and movement of the perpetually presented pop relic. Not wanting to foul his stereo with the drippy dead man goo on his rubber-gloved hands, Don reaches his elbow toward the volume knob—cranking up the tune while serenading the cleaned-up corpse in an off-key sing-a-long.

As the song ends, Don turns off the radio and reviews his handiwork. Disturbingly, the tall, white, middle-aged man with receding grey-brown hair laid out on his table looks much like himself. The paunch of front belly, side belly,

and gravity-humbled breast blubber hanging on the body cause Don to look down and pinch his own puffy pads.

"Time for group, chubby," he says to the stiff, as he grabs his coat and makes his way to the rear exit of Goodrich Mortuary Services.

When he arrives at Pilgrim Lutheran in his shiny, 2004 "Eagle Coach" Lincoln hearse, Don checks his watch: 2:45 PM on the dot. He's fifteen minutes early, same as every Saturday. Plenty of time to set up the folding chairs and, most importantly for Don, to claim his special spot in the center of the church basement. He places a memory foam cushion on the cleanest chair he can find and greets people from his Goldilocks position as they slowly filter into the small, wood-paneled room.

Though Don never says much, the fact that he's there holding down the same seat each week has a comforting effect on regulars and newcomers alike. No matter what troubling inconsistencies plague their lives, there's always Don, sitting there with his beige slacks, loafers, and blue button-down shirt—well-manicured in every way—offering reassuring nods, waves, and smiles to everyone who enters. He's been coming to the Saturday afternoon gatherings for over twenty years, making Don the longest standing member, not just of the current recovery group,

Overeaters Anonymous, but of every 12 Step fellowship that has congregated in Pilgrim Lutheran's basement before them.

When Don first started coming, it was Narcotics Anonymous who held the 3 PM Saturday slot. In those days, Don had been experimenting with "sherm," as embalming fluid laced cigarettes are known on the street.

"An occupational hazard if ever there was one," he often said in meetings.

Don soon found that attending NA gave him a sense of purpose and belonging unlike anything he had previously experienced in life. In no time, he had adopted the 12 Step lingo and taken a commitment setting up chairs and making coffee. People appreciated that Don came early each week, sometimes even bringing donuts or cookies. Good old Don. An addict who had really turned his life around. An inspiration to newcomers and old-timers alike.

One Saturday afternoon, three years after Don joined the group, Pilgrim Lutheran's pastor came downstairs and asked Narcotics Anonymous and its members to leave the premises immediately and permanently. The church elders, he'd said, were fed up with finding hypodermic needles and glassine baggies in Pilgrim Lutheran's bathrooms, pews, and parking lot.

"We have children here. Children!" the pastor had exclaimed.

As other group members sauntered out of the basement discussing which NA meetings they might disperse to, Don sat motionless, holding tightly to his plastic folding chair. The locations others mentioned sounded so far away—not just geographically, but emotionally. Don couldn't imagine abandoning his station. That particular spot in that particular church basement was where he had learned to listen to the troubles of others and had, on occasion, even shared a bit of his own. It was his place of ease and his place of power. It was the one place in life where the world settled perfectly around him.

And it wasn't just Don who knew it. Other attendees referred to the center seat as "Don's spot" as well. The secretary even called on people during the meeting's sharing time in terms of their proximity to the group's most devout member. "Guy next to Don," or "Lady behind Don," he sometimes said. And it wasn't only the people. The fluorescent lights, wood paneling, chipped linoleum floor, folding chairs, and coffee machine seemed to understand Don and his place in the room as well. So it took a few moments to understand Pilgrim Lutheran's pastor when he said,

"I'm talking to *you*, mister," while he looked sharply at Don, the room's last holdout, with a stiff arm and a long finger pointing toward the exit.

Luckily for Don, it was just three weeks later that a sign for Alcoholics Anonymous appeared on Pilgrim Lutheran's back door. He was more than happy to "keep coming back"—as the famous end-of-meeting chant instructed—not at all concerned that the focus of sessions had shifted from drugs to booze. It was no problem for Don to take the first step—admitting his powerlessness over alcohol—when he considered the time he had awoken to find permanent marker penises scribbled all over him after a drunken dorm party. Though the physical and emotional hangovers he experienced his first year at college kept him from ever drinking again, Don was certain, particularly after joining AA, that he had a latent condition when it came to alcohol.

As before, Don showed up early each week to place chairs and power the percolator. He studied AA's Big Book and quickly picked up the verbiage of the recovering alcoholic. Other group members appreciated that Don utilized well-worn one-liners during his brief shares, like "put the plug in the jug," "keep an attitude of gratitude," and "I suffer from alcohol*ism*, not alcohol-*wasm*." He was one of the good guys. A true alcoholic in recovery. Someone to look up to.

After sixteen years of one drunk helping another, the Saturday afternoon AA group had outgrown the little basement room and found a larger locale on the other side of Saint Paul. As previously, Don didn't leave with the others but instead kept his long-settled spot in the bowels of that particular building. Because Pilgrim Lutheran's basement had become a sought-after recovery room, it was just one week later that another 12 Step group took over the Saturday slot: Gamblers Anonymous.

It was no problem for Don to "qualify" for GA when he thought back to his Las Vegas elopement with Dolores—a woman he'd fallen hard and fast in love with after hooking up with her on his embalming table during a Goodrich funeral service ten years previous.

On the second night of their honeymoon, Dolores came down with a migraine and insisted Don go to their scheduled Englebert Humperdinck show alone.

"Front row seats, Don. You gotta go," she said.

Though he preferred not to leave her side, Don did as instructed. Less than halfway through the performance, however, he thought it best to return to the hotel with two pints of Dolores' favorite ice cream. He crept quietly into the room and was just about to say "surprise" when he heard grunting. Stepping further in, Don saw a tan, naked man with a giant pompadour wig doggy-styling his beloved bride on their California king honeymoon bed. Ketchup-stained food wrappers and bottles of cheap booze littered the giant mattress, framing the corrupt couple like a lurid laurel wreath. Neither Dolores nor the Elvis-impersonating-wedding-officiant who'd married them the day before heard Don standing near the bathroom muttering "no" under his breath while they did the dirty deed. As he felt his heart sink through his body and fall all of the hotel's thirty-two floors down to street level, Don slipped out of the room, placed the Ben and Jerry's by the door, and disappeared into the least inhabited corner of the casino.

After dropping over five hundred and fifty dollars in quarter slots at the Stardust that night, he caught an early flight back to St. Paul, had a lawyer draw up annulment papers, and swore off relationships for good.

At GA, Don set up the chairs and made coffee as he'd done previously. No one in the meetings pried into the details of his compulsive gambling. It was enough that they saw the hangdog look on his face when he alluded to his "deplorable past actions." In any event, the base-

ment's new anonymous crew dissolved after just three months due to a lack of financial stability as the pass-the-basket money disappeared each week into the pocket of one desperate soul or another.

Two weeks later, in late October of that year, the 3 PM Saturday spot was filled by its first foreign language group: Neuróticos Anónimos.

*Great opportunity to practice the old High School Spanish,* Don had thought, though "Mi nombre es Don y soy neurótico" was the most he felt comfortable saying out loud at meetings.

As per usual, Don came early for set up. The small, mostly male congregation, greeted Don warmly, happy to have the gringo mascot in their midst, especially considering what a buena taza de café he made.

Although Don didn't believe himself to be burdened by neurosis when he joined the ill-at-ease Latinos, he soon found that he couldn't stop scribbling his first name as *Dón*—with an accent mark above the o—over and over again inside the spiral notebooks that he'd begun bringing to group. The repeated Dón doodling somehow made him feel closer to the others, no matter that it was not the correct Spanish spelling of his name.

The neuróticos meeting, never very large to begin with, began to shrink in numbers as Winter set in. Eventually, only two people remained: non-Spanish-speaking Don and a short, bald man with a robust facial tic named Juan José. Unable to understand his Hispanic counterpart's hour-long monologues during the two-man tenure of Neuróticos Anonimos, Don instead focused on the twitch that zig-zagged from scalp to chin and back again across Juan José's face during the brief moments he stopped speaking. The remarkable feat of facial dexterity was an inspiration to Don who practiced his own eye jerks, nose wiggles, and mouth contortions in the mortuary mirror each week between meetings—sometimes even performing the well-rehearsed facial oscillations for departed souls in Goodrich's lower level while preparing them for their final journey.

As for Juan José, it had been no problem that the gringo Don was the only other attendee of the recovery sessions, but the cold weather and lack of proper heating in the church basement was another thing. As brutal January temperatures froze the city of Saint Paul that winter, the group's last Spanish speaker and his unusual spasm finally stopped making the chilly trek to Pilgrim Lutheran, leaving Don without a single neurótico to make coffee for.

After Juan José's departure, Don continued stopping by the church basement each Saturday to check on its 12 Step status. Sometimes he even went in, set up a few chairs, and sat alone thinking about his former anonymous allies—wondering where they were and who was making coffee for them.

As the room remained empty week after week, depression sent Don down a dark path. Though he fantasized about drinking beer, playing the slots at Mystic Lake Casino, or even smoking a little sherm, Don instead succumbed to what he deemed the least harmful addiction in his repertoire: filling spiral notebooks with the word *Dón* while chanting "Mi nombre es Don y soy neurótico."

One Saturday, at the beginning of Spring, when Don was driving by Pilgrim Lutheran with his notebooks, he noticed a sandwich sign set outside the church's back door that read: *Overeaters Anonymous meeting today, 3pm.* Excitedly, he parked his hearse in the church lot, chuckling as he thought about the term *sandwich sign* together with the word *overeater* and then quickly correcting himself for being judgmental.

As he got out of the car, Don pulled the waistband of his beige slacks down slightly, letting his belly protrude a bit.

"Oh yeah," he said, rubbing his newly freed paunch. "I'm a natural for this."

The first few weeks in OA were a dream. Don memorized the names of regulars and picked up the group's style and vernacular quickly. The overeaters were comforted by his presence and appreciated his setup skills, though they asked him to please not bring snacks. More than ever,

Don fit right in. And best of all there was no sign of the "Big Bummer."

The thing is, Don was not the only one who had kept coming back through Pilgrim Lutheran's many 12 Step transitions. There was another man who'd frequented the basement during those twenty-plus years.

"Name's Ralph an' I'm a *attic*," he had introduced himself loudly at his first Narcotics Anonymous meeting.

Don was immediately rankled by the newcomer who was opposite to himself in every way. Where Don was consistently early, Ralph was always late. Where Don sat in the same spot every session, Ralph moved from place to place—now in the front, now in the back, now standing up, now sitting down—even shifting spots several times during an individual meeting. And where Don showed up for group each week—even if it meant occasionally hiring another funeral director to officiate a service—Ralph came and went, sometimes disappearing for a month or more at a time.

While the man's tardiness, lack of commitment, and inability to pick a permanent place had been irksome to Don, Ralph's sloppy clothes, bad personal hygiene, and repeated interruptions of personal shares had been even more annoying. There were other issues too: Ralph drinking more than his share of the coffee, never contributing when the basket was passed, brazenly flirting with the group's women, and, most painfully for Don, his perpetual misquoting of the renowned end-of-meeting slogan: "Keep coming back, it works *if you're worth it.*"

On top of all that, Ralph badly imitated the addictions of whichever 12 Step tenant occupied the basement, declaring compulsions he seemed to have just come down with. In NA, he presented a paint-huffing problem. In AA, he proclaimed his powerlessness over Bailey's Irish Cream. In GA, he disclosed an inability to stop dropping dollars at the dog tracks. Don, suspecting the Big Bummer of being a big phony, wished the man would leave the recovery room to the addicts who needed it. With the arrival of the neuróticos, Don's wish came true.

"Wonder how you say 'so long Big Bummer' in Español," Don laughed, realizing his rival had quit coming back due to a lack of language skills.

The basement remained entirely Ralph-free through the neuróticos run and exactly four weeks into the overeater's takeover. At OA's fifth meeting, though, Ralph reemerged, waving cheerily at Don as he waded through the room well after the session had begun. Don winced, noticing that his nemesis had put on a little weight since last he'd seen him.

"Trying too hard to fit in . . . as always," Don thought. "An even *bigger* bummer than before."

And so it was, much to Don's displeasure, that Ralph became a semi-regular in the room once again.

After a month of watching Ralph continue to round out week by week, Don became competitive. He started by adding an extra dessert here and there but was soon doubling portions at most meals. Now, three months into OA membership, and twenty-five pounds heavier, Don is more certain than ever that this particular group in this particular place is where he truly belongs.

As the last of the overeaters take their seats, Don checks his watch again: 3 PM on the button. He drowsily closes his eyes, hoping the Big Bummer won't show up today. It isn't until the sharing portion of group is well underway that he's awakened.

"I know what you're talkin' 'bout, Pam. Them *Dairy Queens* is a big trigger for me too . . ." Ralph says loudly, interrupting the woman next to him.

Don jerks up at hearing his adversary's nasally voice fill the room. He thinks back to the Big Bummer jibber-jabbering at him near the bathroom two weeks earlier.

"Look, I need a sponsor and you're the only guy here with real time under his belt. I wanna be more like you, Don . . ."

It was horrifying to hear at first, but the more Don thought about it, the more he realized it *would* be good if Ralph were more like him—clean, quiet, punctual—especially considering

the unkempt man wasn't likely to leave the Saturday support group anytime soon.

Though he finally agreed to take on the role, it wasn't clear to Don which 12 Step program he should mentor Ralph in. Never having had a sponsor himself, he figured the best bet would be to point his would-be pupil toward the proper literature—leaving it to the wisdom of the written word to cure his chaotic counterpart. Don picked his favorite self-help bookstore, *Endless Evolution*, for their first meeting to take place, setting the date for this Saturday after group.

M eagan Sullivan arrives at *Endless Evolution* to meet her sponsor, Katrina, after their Saturday afternoon Al-Anon group—same as every week. It's a ritual both have come to appreciate since they started working together six months ago. But at a recent Co-Dependents Anonymous meeting—Meagan's seventh 12 Step affiliation since beginning her path to recovery—she was told by long time group members that having a sponsor is simply "too co-dependent" for someone with problems like hers. Though the words rang true for Meagan, her difficulty with confrontation has kept her from letting go of the many mentors she has in various sex, love, and debt addiction groups. She figures it will be easiest to rid herself of those other relationships if she can first fire her closest sponsor, Katrina.

As Katrina's yellow VW pulls up, Meagan twists her mouth into an overly excited smile and waves emphatically.

"So, how's it going with Step Four?" Katrina invites, as they walk toward the bookstore's coffee bar.

"Yeah . . . I'm still working on it," Meagan says.

"Don't want to get stuck there, girl. Put all those gory details onto paper and let's talk it out. That's when things start to change. You'll see."

"I know . . ." Meagan says, listlessly as she does a quick scan of the room. "There's a couple of books I want to pick up today. Meet you up front in a few?"

"That's my girl, always looking for more support," Katrina says encouragingly as she picks up her latte and moves toward the newly expanded 'Incense and Candles' section of the store.

"Hey, Don."

"Oh . . . hi, Ralph," Don says drably, tucking a book entitled *Overcoming Obesity in Obtainable Ways* back into its nook and checking his watch.

"Sorry, I'm a little late," Ralph says with a shrug.

"You might be interested to know they have an entire section here dedicated to punctuality," Don says.

"Had to stop for gas. And then the traffic . . ." Ralph starts to explain.

"As you've likely heard in the rooms, you need a spiritual solution to your malady," Don interrupts, pausing to let the words of wisdom sink in.

Ralph is about to speak when Don starts again,

"This store has many fine selections to help with all sorts of *maladies*. And because your maladies are going to be different than mine, you should take a look around and see if there's something suitable for you. I assume you already have the 12 Step literature?"

"You bet. And I'm ready to jump in . . ."

"Whoa . . . hold your horses. Let's not get ahead of ourselves. How about you first figure out your top three or four *maladies* and see if you can find some books here that address them."

Seeing his sponsee's hesitation Don offers another thought.

"Or . . . you can simply wander the store and see what speaks to you, as I often do."

Don begins a slow walk through the store with Ralph trailing behind. After passing rows of books on self-improvement, self-empowerment, and self-development, astrology, numerology, and parapsychology, ascended masters, Zen masters, mastering oneself, and meeting one's shadow, Don finally comes to a halt at an endcap rack of half-priced recordings sitting in front of a CD listening station.

"Oh yes!" Don exclaims, picking out an audio series and wagging it at Ralph's eye level. "This is very good. *And well priced.*"

Ralph leans in to read the title:

*What Do You Hope To Gain From Your Life? — An audio series by renowned life strategist John Lynwood.*

Ralph takes the CD and stares at it blankly.

"And look, it's already in the listening station so you can *try before you buy*," Don says, pointing at a pair of headphones hanging from the CD stand.

As Don follows his malady-intuition back down the book aisles, Ralph turns, bumping into a curvy woman with dyed red hair and cat eye glasses putting on a pair of headphones at the listening station next to his.

"Hey. Wow. Didn't see you. Maybe I need glasses too, haha," Ralph says awkwardly.

The woman smiles intensely but doesn't speak. Ralph, unsure of what's happening, smiles back, puts on a headset and holds up the John Lynwood CD. The redhead holds up the same CD and nods in affirmation. They press play simultaneously.

*What do you hope to gain from your life? Let's try that again. What-do-you-hope-to-gain-from-your-life? That's the big question, isn't it?*

Ralph points at the earphones and smiles playfully at the question. The cat glasses lady responds by pooching her lips and raising her eyebrows along with an 'I dunno' shrug.

*To begin with, let's consider each word in the sentence slowly and carefully. 'What' makes it a question. 'Do' makes it an action. 'You,' it's all about your personal journey. 'Hope,' the dreams that are hidden underneath, desperately waiting to be fulfilled . . .*

At the word "hope," the woman nonchalantly undoes the three top buttons on her vintage blouse. Ralph's eyes widen.

*'To,' a direction or movement forward. 'Gain,' more than there is now.*

Playfully undoing a fourth button, the woman looks down at the swelling lump in Ralph's pants.

*'From,'* the opposite of *to*—we'll speak more on the power of combining opposites later.

Ralph glances nervously around the room as the woman suddenly seizes his zipper.

*'Your,"* it inherently belongs to you. *'Life,'* something that exists.

Ralph watches speechlessly as she spits in one hand and pulls out his penis with the other.

*Altogether you have a question, an action, a journey, the hidden dreams waiting to become known, the movement that takes one forward, abundance, the powerful opposites, the inheritance, and finally . . . the spectacular movement from the energetic realm into full existence.*

After a few gentle strokes, Ralph grimaces and stifles a shriek while the henna-haired hottie expertly side-steps the squirting semen emitting from his member.

*Now, let's repeat the question. What do you hope to gain from your life? Let this query work its way through you. Give over to what arises within . . .*

As Ralph finishes zipping his pants, he looks up to see the woman has already started walking away.

"Miss . . . can I call you?" he asks, as he hangs up the headphones.

"What you did in there . . ." Katrina says, pulling Meagan out of the bookstore.

"I know, I'm so sorry . . ." Meagan says in a little girl voice.

Two men step out of *Endless Evolution*, interrupting the women's conversation. Meagan pretends not to recognize the one waving weakly in her direction. Once the men turn toward the parking lot, Katrina continues,

"There's no point in taking you through the steps if you're just going to act out like that . . . in *public!*"

After Katrina storms off, Meagan smiles to herself, happy to have taken the first step in working out her co-dependency issues.

Don digs into a double-order Long John Silver's Fish and Chips platter sitting on the embalming table.

"At least it's not burgers," he tells himself.

After the last bite, he washes his hands thoroughly in the slop sink, turns on the oldies station and pulls on a pair of rubber gloves. As he gets back to work on the body, the strummy guitar intro to *Peaceful Easy Feeling* by The Eagles comes on.

"Oh, *yeah* . . ." Don says, reaching his elbow toward the volume knob, feeling how perfectly the middle-of-the-road pop melody matches his mood.

Don hums along as he matches the cadaver's hair to a mall-style glamor shot lying on its chest.

*It's good to be a sponsor*, he thinks.

When the song comes to an end, Don shuts off the radio and focuses on his last stage of prep. Carefully, he wires the mouth shut and adds caps under the eyelids to ensure they'll remain closed from here on in, or at least until the body is deep in the ground.

JULIAN GEORGE

# FIN DE PARTIE

*To be read aloud in a generic Southern accent, more William Faulkner than Foghorn Leghorn if you please, but only if you can manage, otherwise...*

What an absurd way to die, in the bath, going down slow, absurd as the way he had lived.

Nothing to be done. No feeling in the limbs. Though cognisant, he was unable to call out for help, and wouldn't have bothered if he could, truth be told.

Out of time, out of mind. Born too soon. A superfluous man, a Monsieur Je Ne Sais Quoi. Unsputed master of a silly, meaningless game. child's play. A mere pastime, something to keep him diverted before he came of age and could take up the law.

The fuss on his return from Europe! Embarrassing. Out of all proportion to his actual achievements. Parades and brass bands, the solemn speeches and oppressive banquets, the presumptuous newspapermen he was well shot of, the false friends.

Every gladhanding speculator in the land, from sea to shining sea, sidling up to him with a proposition, we'll make a mint, son, me and you, just requires a little showmanship on your part, a little give, what do you say? We'll work out the details later.

As if he accepted money for playing. Lend his good name to a cigar or brand of bourbon whisky. 'Perform'.

They no more knew him than the Man on the Moon.

After all the corn and hollering hooray, home to 417 Royal Street . . . and nothing.

Unable to make a go of the Bar, our Napoleon, our Alexander, his shingle invisible to passersby, our Belisarius as well, so to speak.

Then there was the issue of the war. He could not make up his mind whether to serve the Union or rebel with the Confederacy. Though he opposed secession and could not abide slavery, a vile institution, he could not turn his back on Louisiana. No. Never.

He took himself off to Paris, followed the carnage in French and English periodicals. There were trips to Havana, which was not a million miles away from his beloved New Orleans.

After Sherman's March to the Sea, hell on earth he gathered, he returned to a city swarming with carpetbaggers . . .

To the pitying looks of fair-eyed ladies who once would have welcomed his declarations with blushing consent . . .

To the eye-rolling gentlemen who crossed the street to avoid him, loathe to be drawn into yet another meandering chinwag about how his brother-in-law was out to steal his patrimony,

an outlandish notion belied by his dapper appearance—a monocle!—and public knowledge. That and very likely they were still mad at his 'playing Hamlet' over the war.

That neither Blue nor Gray would have an 'in-between man' front or behind lines was neither here nor there. Need I remind you, sir, 'They also serve who only stand and wait'?

The cheek. Every last one of these fancy dans a colonel this, that and the other. Medals. So many medals. One could go blind from so many medals. Medals for the smartest uniform. For knowing how to handle cutlery in the English manner. Medals for mixing up Shakespeare and Milton.

Not a one faced fire. Mercifully, New Orleans was spared Vicksburg's fate.

Is that the time? My mother and sister await, sir, *à table* you understand. Must be off, mustn't be late. Good day to you, sir, good day.

Too much commerce of this kind can be dispiriting.

Time came when the only living soul he could bring himself to talk to was himself, excitable confabs that drained him and alarmed others. Fact.

He broke down for good finally, a gibbering wreck, and stayed home curled up in bed, buried under blankets in the heat, waiting for the flag to fall, the end of the world, the death of a mouse.

His mother and sister on tiptoe, taking pains to care for him, an invalid lost to mental strife, trays of food left untouched.

As he slipped away, a stirring image saw him out, of men dressed in black and red climbing a broad staircase, to the sound of trumpets.

P aul Morphy vs The Duke of Brunswick and Count Isouard, played in a box at the Paris Opéra, 1858, Philidor Defence 1 e4 e5 2 Nf3 d6 3 d4 Bg4 4 dxe5 Bxf3 5 Qxf3 dxe5 6 Bc4 Nf6 7 Qb3 Qe7 8 Nc3 c6 9 Bg5 b5? 10 Nxb5 cxb5 11 Bxb5+ Nbd7 12 0-0-0 Rd8 13 Rxd7 Rxd7 14 Rd1 Qe6 15 Bxd7+ Nxd7 16 Qb8+ Nxb8 17 Rd8 mate.

Laura Givens

# you ever hear a maraca baby

Thought the good thing about a rattlesnake was at least they warn you, but this one didn't, not 'til after.

I know baby you told me.

Can't blame her though, least I don't blame her. I'm in her home for all she knows I'm there to stomp up her house or steal her babies so what else can she do. But I sure wish she'd warned me you know?

I know, but it wasn't your fault.

No, I got in her way, I did. Of course she's got that rattle. It works fine I heard it. Just wish she'd used it a little sooner is all.

Don't matter now

> he says as they make their way south-south-east to an old gold rush ghost town called San Luis or San Ruiz. Where there might be a clinic or at least a pharmacy and a doctor or maybe a nurse who has dealt with this sort of thing before and knows just what to do.

You think I oughta take my shoe off? I can't see my ankle anyway must be—oh don't look don't look—keep driving. I think I gotta take the shoe off.

I don't know maybe pressure's good maybe you should keep it on.

I don't know it hurts I'm gonna take it off otherwise they'll have to cut if off and I just got these.

Well don't worry about the shoes! Christ! We can buy shoes. But if it hurts maybe you should take it off.

Ohhh lord this hurts like a mother. But it don't look so bad, kinda like a sprain—well like a bad sprain I guess.

Well that's good maybe.

Well I'm not saying drive slower, I'm just saying I'm glad I took the shoe off.

Her foot continues to swell. Parts of it begin to look almost bruised, especially around the toes, shapeless now, smashed together, unbendable. Her stretched-thin skin reminds her of a fish bladder. She wants to touch it, press a fingertip into it, watch as it dimples or resists. She keeps her hands in her lap and says

You know I saw on TV, on . . . oh what show was it? They were talking about how you don't really feel things when they happen. Which of course you do. Of course you touch a hot stove you feel that, but they were saying how right at first you don't really. Or you feel it but you don't know you feel it? Like only your hand knows? And then it takes the rest of you a while to catch up. Does that sound right to you? I mean I know people on TV lie sometimes, I know that, but babe I didn't feel it at first I didn't even feel it for

You felt it honey, you just didn't know it was a snake.

That's what they were saying. You do feel it kind of but you don't *know* what you feel. Like we think we're this *one thing*, but we're not, we're a million things just trying to catch up with each other. Like this leg of mine it knows. It knows whether or not I'm dying and it's trying to tell me but I can't understand it all I know is it hurts but. Maybe I should take an aspirin or something we got any aspirin?

No you can't take aspirin, it thins the blood. But we'll be there soon just hang on just think about something else.

You think I'll lose my leg?

Something nice, think about something nice.

I saw this Iraq war vet on TV he lost both his legs. Didn't matter. I mean it mattered but he didn't let it stop him or slow him down. He did everything even went rock climbing. But he said the thing he couldn't get over were the phantom pains. Phantom pains can you explain that to me? How my leg an hour ago was a perfect leg and it takes its sweet time to feel a snake bite and then tomorrow I have no leg at all and it might still hurt like it does now like a universe of pain seeping out from her calf up and into and through her so that she is infused with it every part of her a little bit on fire. She closes her eyes and searches inside for even a tiny place within her that isn't burning. He says

Just breathe through it baby, I told you think about nice things. Calm things. Easy things. Think about that trip to Hawaii I'm gonna take you on once we

Oh it feels real bad oh jesus

You gotta hold on ok? We're almost there pretty soon it won't even feel like a mosquito bite. Try not to worry just think about the two of us on an island, with blue skies, big old clouds, the ocean all around us. The whole Pacific so close that even when we can't see it we can still hear it, nice and relaxing, the waves just rolling over the rocks and the sand like on those sleep tapes you like. We'll stay in one of those cabanas right on the beach, nothing to do but drink mai tais and walk along the shore, maybe find a palm tree to sit under. You see it? Just the two of us, maybe a hula girl

Maybe a hula guy with her

And a hula guy too. Just playing their ukuleles and singing a nice song for us while we watch the waves roll in go on try to picture it, close your eyes now.

Which she does. Right when they pass the bright orange on green sign saying DE-TOUR BRIDGE CLOSED AHEAD that maybe she wouldn't have seen anyway. The sign is big enough, but he doesn't see it either. He keeps his eyes on her face, still beautiful, but a little flushed, ragged,

like she's walking up a steep hill. She sits quietly and tries to think nice thoughts like *blue skies* only it's not working all she can picture is the brown-black-grey snake behind her on the path, wrapped around itself, calm and so small really. She thinks *cabana ocean waves* but just sees the two tiny puncture wounds above her ankle barely bleeding at all but undeniably there. She thinks *palm tree hula ukulele* but all she hears is the snake's belated rattle loud and clear, like a toy maraca she had when she was little.

You know that rattlesnake sounded just like you said it would. Remember you told me what to listen for, what to watch out for, you told me baby.

I know I did but I didn't explain right, they don't always make a sound. I shoulda told you.

No I shoulda paid attention, stayed out of her way. Poor snake.

Quiet enough now, in the bed of their pickup. What is left of her at least, after being shot at, then trampled, then crushed by the monsters, for no reason she could have ever made sense of, even if they'd bothered to explain.

You think maybe she didn't even have a choice? I mean, you think maybe I scared her and she bit me and then she realized she bit me so she couldn't even warn me until it was too late? I'm glad she tried I just wish she'd done it sooner is all.

I know baby, I know.

# Bridge 101

## Friday, October 14th

Spent the morning issuing bits and watching the weight gauge turn from green to blue and then back to green again, which it will remain for the rest of the day. Returning traffic is always dribs and drabs.

The gauge is a lot of nothing in my opinion. This bridge was reinforced with 'ten acre widths of steel', or so I remember hearing over and over on the radio. How could there be any risk? I think the blue 'dangerous load' light is only there to keep the operators in a state of high anxiety during the morning rush and working faster for it. Well, it doesn't hold sway over me, I can tell you that for nothing. I issue as fast as I like to and no faster.

Perhaps the bridge is made of old plywood. This wouldn't surprise me. I was going to say nothing surprises me, but surely something could.

I ate lunch alone in my booth, which I still hate. After they started with the new lunchtimes I made a deal with Randall that we would take turns keeping each other company. We only tried this once. Randall came through so heavily interlaced I could barely make him out. It was pointless anyway, what with him having to maintain his window at the same time. Randall has deep level fear, I only have simple level, so he may well have been pleased to not have to have lunch with company anymore. This is something he would never tell me.

## Monday, October 17th

Average weekend. Mostly in the environs of the orchard. Didn't really hang out with anyone. I approached a few friendly pods but felt too restless to wait the loading times. Too bored to be alone, too impatient to join in. I made myself smile, to myself, about this, despite not finding it properly amusing. I did see Randall, who I

spotted and briefly spoke to up by the illuminated basins. And I asked him if he fancied a drink outside of the orchard, but he said it wouldn't be possible.

'Why not?' I said.

'Oh, you know,' said Randall. 'Just need to stay close to home.'

'Why?' I said. And then, 'only messing about.'

Randall never says a real goodbye, but I know he's about to disconnect when he starts sighing and humming little intervals to himself. Afterwards I watched his likeness float away from me across the water and up towards the rippled crest that borders the association area.

There was a lot of transport this morning, especially heavy carriers, and my gauge was glowing dark blue. I thought about Randall to pacify myself. I wonder if in doing this I transmit my stresses onto him through the walls. In which case, what do I receive from the walls? Quiet, I suppose. Quiet and peace.

In the afternoon I filled a notebook with strange symbols and tried to write Randall a poem illustrating how I feel, but I only managed one line: 'In golden light I dance my joy away.' Will write a second line when one occurs to me.

## Tuesday October 18th

So far has been quite an easy day. As I'm writing this I'm eating a spinach and feta thing and planning little parties in my mind. It's Randall's birthday on Thursday and I want to do something special for him. He doesn't even like people to mention it, let alone commune in his honour, but I don't think he knows what he likes. He just puts up a general protest against anything more vibrant than gentle conversation. It's boring, really, when you think of all the fun we could be having.

Last night I went into the orchard for my weekly memory group. Willow-chair kept speaking over me. I complained but the therapist wasn't interested.

'Willow-chair is simply confirming your journey.'

This has happened before and specifically with willow-chair. Maybe they aren't rotating us as much they're supposed to. When we deliver our stories I try to catch the therapist out by changing tiny details about my family, such as that me and Peter shared a bedroom that faced north-east rather than north-west, but she always picks me up on them. She doesn't notice if you relay the events of your life out of order. Last week I said Dad had dropped me down the stairs the day after I got banished from a housing co-op for repeatedly leaving the outer gates unlocked. Afterwards the therapist praised me for how I'd performed in the session. For how connected I now was to my personal history.

## Wednesday October 19th

Busy on the bridge this morning. More transport than ever. It's because the trains aren't running into the city, or as regularly, or else are all broken. Something like that. I heard a manager talking about it on my break. I find it hard to pay attention to anything about the city. I wonder what the centre looks like now. The suburbs can't have changed that much.

There used to be a city simulation in the orchard, but they stopped updating it years ago. I only accessed it once. I'd thought it might be too depressing to see, but then I chided myself for being negative, and went to it. Was so awful. Far worse than I'd worried even. I should trust my instincts sometimes. But when?

Not sure I'll know anyone from my area when I move back. Peter's still there, I would guess, although he probably still won't talk to me. He never liked Randall. Nor me, let's be honest amongst ourselves, but he appreciated my subservience until he'd lost it. And there was a lot of talk of upheaval and shame but that was more the rankle, I feel sure of that.

Sometimes when I'm on shift I consider that I no longer answer to Peter and I gasp about it with something like pleasure. That he no longer breathes down my neck, as they say. And I know I now answer to the managers instead, but this doesn't bother me a great deal. Because as long as I issue a few bits here and there, and remain in my booth for the duration of my hours, they don't have an opinion on what I do. I could be sat hallucinating wild grey infinities all day, it wouldn't matter to them. It doesn't.

I'll find a house in the old area, after I leave here. One with a large window. This is our plan. I'll grow herbs on the windowsill to make use of the light. And I won't need to do much else besides attending to the herbs, because I will have been handsomely compensated. And I'll wait for Randall, for when he gets there.

After work I decided against going into the orchard. I don't always have to. It's Randall's birthday tomorrow and I was happy enough just sitting in my chair and thinking about that. I hope he's excited for it, too.

Peter's birthday is three days before mine, and when we were children they were always celebrated together, on my birthday. I always disliked that. I feel silly moaning about this now, but I still feel resentful. Maybe I could place all my resentments in my hair and then cut it all off and throw it over the bridge. There would be no downside to this.

## Thursday October 20th

Randall was very cruel to me today. I had it near enough agreed with the managers that a few of us would be allowed to surprise him on his lunch break with some sweets and ribbons and a bottle of wine I'd been saving for the occasion. Red wine, which had actually been a thank you gift from Randall, but so long ago I didn't think he'd remember. So around midday a little troop of us went over to his booth. Randall wouldn't even come to the door. I tried to speak to him in a soft and calming voice but he shouted back at me through the hatch that I should leave him alone and stop pestering him. I was giving him a party! What sort of pestering is that? I suggested that maybe he was just shy, and that if he liked it could be just me who he let inside. He said that he'd rather it be just me who he didn't, and I threw the bottle of wine at his window, causing him to duck.

'It's not going to break the glass, you fucking idiot!' I said. I regret saying that. Tomorrow there's going to be a meeting with Randall and the managers to straighten things out. It will be good to clear the air. I really don't know why he's behaving like this at the moment.

In the evening I made soup and ate it in the orchard sat on the slopes. I watched a few of the films. I didn't pay attention to them. In honesty I was mainly there to try and apologise to Randall, who goes there most evenings. He never showed up. Or else he's blocked me. Which just seems crazy, as he has no reason to. Hopefully he was just offline. Seems a dreadful way to spend your birthday, but there you go.

## Friday October 21st

Today was the worst day I've had for a very long time. I couldn't sleep last night for guilt, and early morning in the booth was more punishing than ever. The bridge was so busy that the blue light on the weight gauge moved from constant to a flashing state I've never seen before. I confess I did work faster as a result.

After my break I was summoned to a meeting room and met by a couple of managers. Horrible ones. They all are, I suppose. I asked them where Randall was, and they said he wasn't coming. I asked them why and they told me that Randall had been released. I asked them if he'd left me any instructions about changes to our arrangement. Because it's supposed to be me who gets out first. I've made Randall go over it a hundred times. And not because I need reminding, but I like to hear him say it. And I'm going home first. That's how the plan starts, for heaven's sake! In order that I can find a house for us to live in. With a window so vast you could cultivate a whole garden at the base of it. Our booths ha▮ meagre windows, you understand, and so it w▮ be a great relief to us to have one so impressiv▮ And when we entertain guests they will star▮ rapt in front of it. And when they complime▮ the window we will receive it as our own succes▮ And it will fill us up with pride.

One of the managers offered me a cup of h▮ chocolate. I asked if we could get Randall on t▮ phone, and just get everything sorted. I desire▮ things to be sorted out.

They said I must forget about Randall. He▮ gone now. And that I was to stay for longer stil▮ on account of the bottle of wine. They asked m▮ where it had come from, and I screamed an▮ kicked and uselessly tried to get at them, and▮ said they were the scum of the earth and nothin▮ else.

## Monday 24th October

Average weekend. Nothing much to report. I di▮ a few loops of the orchard but didn't really cha▮ to anyone. I slept and woke again and ate mor▮ soup. Near solid traffic this morning. The blu▮ light has been flashing faster, strobing almost.

I thought about asking the managers for Ran▮ dall's address in town, but I don't think they'▮ know it, or else wouldn't give it to me, whic▮ works out the same.

I'll need it, though, for when I get out. Other▮ wise I won't know where I'm headed to.

Tonight I might go into the orchard and sit o▮ the slopes. The managers might have lied▮ Maybe Randall will be there tonight. He doe▮ tend to go there in the evenings.

Thought of a second line for my poem: 'Th▮ joy I've lost is hidden in the sky'.

34

*EXACTING CLAM*

Ian Boulton

# Triptych-on-Sea

## Panel One: *Beside myself with glee*

All we are looking for—all we are ever looking for, honestly—is a little illumination, some light to ease our way down this dark narrow path. We are not greedy and our ambitions are modest. So, bearing that in mind, do you think it would be, as it were, *enlightening* to have a sneakful (?) peek at her search history?

There's bound to be lots of the usual.

*When does absent mindedness become dementia*

*Is light headedness when putting on shoes an indication of a propensity to strokes*

No need for question marks; if you are searching for answers then all punctuation is implied.

And some that, we imagine, will be very specifically hers.

*What are the obvious signs of pedantry*

*What is the etiquette when correcting someone's English*

*Are standards dropping in schools*

*In public*

*In the home*

Also on her phone there appeared to be an app that she used for taking notes, for jotting down those random thoughts that occurred to her when she sat in that hateful little coffee shop or stared at the blank wall above her television set. There were hundreds of these things, we can say with almost certainty. From time to time we have seen Gillian flicking through them, often visibly appalled at the rubbish she had thought worthy of being recorded. Occasionally—we can say it because we know she never would—she impressed herself. Was that really me? That's quite clever. The look on her face, though she tried to hide it, was sinful pride.

Have you ever tried sitting in that coffee bar on the beach? We can't stand it—weird claustrophobic tiny place, made only more ghastly by the barely audible cool jazz and poppy reggae that drips from its pathetic speakers. Well Gillian, believe it or not, likes it. And it was in that darkened cramped would-be hipster hellhole, sitting amongst the vegan croissants and home-baked pastel de nata (there is a Portuguese mother-in-law somewhere in the management mix), that she sipped her green tea, bag still in the cup, when she had most recently decided to trawl through those past thoughts that she recorded on her phone.

We can just imagine.

*What does a loss of sensation between knee and ankle in the left leg signify*

*Is it possible to have arthritis in only one toe*

*How do you know you are a snob*

We mean you can't even see the sand or the sea from in there, facing, as it does, the back of a few broken down beach huts. Hardly our idea of the perfect space to unwind, but still . . .

That was where she chose to sit the day she cleared her search history—a pity for us as this was a rich (and, we thought, amusing) seam of info but clearly a source of regret or embarrassment for Gillian—and opened that notes app she was so keen on. We have to say that what she read there seemed positively strange to us but clearly our mind works in a very different way to hers. We mean our *minds* work.

*Before I die I really don't want to be interviewed as part of a true crime documentary because somebody I know has killed his wife. You might say that perhaps my wish should be that nobody I know kills their wife but that isn't my fear. Fear needs to be more specific, personal, if we are to be honest. There will never be world peace? Meh. My waist line as of now is the best it's ever going to be? Just kill me. And it's the interview that I dread. This is how I will be remembered: being tangentially connected to some misogynist murdering bastard for all the world to see just because we used to share a car to the garden centre from time to time.*

*Before I die I hope not to be rescued from off a mountainside or out of the sea.*

*Before I die can I please not be forced into making a speech wherein I must say thank you to my parents. Nor do I wish to take any part in a medical trial or be the first to try out some ground-breaking equipment.*

*Before I die I don't want to say sorry more than another thousand times.*

An odd bird, Gillian.

We thought it typical of her that she would jot down what she doesn't want to happen rather than something she does. We often think, when we are thinking of her, why doesn't she just do something? If you are not a joiner, Gillian, we say in our imagined conversation with her, then how can you possibly know what you are not? If you don't pit yourself against your peers then how on Earth can you find out who is better than you? It's all very well showing off, enumerating some ridiculous fantasies that you wish to avoid and, in the process, poking fun at the rest of us, but what is it that you actually want to do?

But she was no hobbyist. Nothing of the kind. We, for example, know from bitter fun experience that we are not poets. Nor are we photographers, athletes of any description, or accomplished pastry chefs. We have actual evidence that we are not potters, water colourists, gifted gardeners, competent morris dancers, socially acceptable salsa dancers, knitters. Ce n'est pas bon, our conversational French. We were Zumba disastrists. That list—more than any thoughts that Gillian might tap into her phone—seemed endless. Our cold water swimming was an embarrassment few would recover from; our quizzing the stuff of legendary ignorance. What skills we do possess, no longer in use, are no match for our non-accomplishments, making for a very uneven ledger: one column what we can do, the other our many failures.

Gillian didn't want to try her hand at amateur dramatics or surfing but . . . we shall say it out loud and therefor force ourselves to go through with it . . . we cannot wait. Even though we know the results are all but inevitable. That's the difference between us and her.

You've noticed, have you, that there are no people around her? There used to be, we're sure. We have a clear memory of stepping aside on the narrow path that leads to our house, making way for her and another.

Was that the impetus for the cat? We have no idea. Maybe altruism is her thing. (Hardly, we can almost hear her saying, bless her.) But shortly after that particular day in the awful café she was walking past one of the charity shops in the High Street (so many of them!) and was taken, seemingly, by a photograph pinned to its message board. Maybe it was goodness on her part or maybe she was making amends for some wrong, who knows? Loneliness even. (A selfish motive then, Gillian would doubtless say, but we think that would be harsh.) But the cat in the picture was soon installed in her home where, as far as we could see, it proved itself to be a little more active than her snow globe from Riga on her windowsill but slightly less so than the giant croton that sat in her conservatory.

She wished she could name the cat Carbury but he already had a name so this is what she whispered to him whilst he sat, immobile, next to her on the sofa. Those times when she had examined the space on the wall above the television had gone. Now she looked down on the sleeping cat beside her. And called him by a name she found distasteful.

One of us understood the Carbury reference by the way; one of us is a philistine.

She could, in all likelihood, come up with hundreds of witty names for animal companions that would bamboozle us both. Gillian is ever so cultured, in case we haven't made that clear. (And where did it get me, we hear her saying, which is, again, typical of her, but still seems an awful shame.)

We went to school together, you know. Not with you, silly, with Gillian. No, you would have remembered us, wouldn't you?

Have we made her sound awful? If so, nostra culpa. She really isn't.

We couldn't stop wondering what she saw in the place so we decided to give it another go. It turned out, as everything always does, to be exactly the same. Barely audible trumpet that may as well be tinnitus dripping into our ears, that view of the unpainted backs of old tatty beach huts, a kitchen argument raging in . . . we want to say Portuguese. God that place is bleak. Why does she keep coming back? What does someone like Gillian see in a place like that? She's a strange one.

On our phone we thought we'd make a few searches.

One of us swore it was Chet Baker.

Fool, the other one said, it's Miles Davis.

How do I go about adopting a retired greyhound

*What are the pros and cons of adopting a retired greyhound*

*What's the worst thing that can happen if you adopt a retired greyhound*

We drank our coffee and nibbled at the tiny little custard tarts.

There was a great deal of chatter, we noticed. Party noises in a radio play. It felt as if we were the freaks, the only ones who didn't get it and that's never, you know, comfortable, is it?

Safe places for our eyes to linger included: coffee surfaces . . . the yellow rim of the saucers . . . ceiling . . . those sad beach huts . . . each other's eyebrows.

Don't fret the black bag is not a dead dog, one of us said.

Don't fret the black bag is not a dead dog, the other said.

Don't fret the black bag is not a dead dog, we said.

And we breathed. We breathed with our mouths like deep sea divers.

And we looked down once more.

Her forehead is the shape of our phone, one of us said.

We looked at it with greater intent, lying between us on the round blue-tiled table.

It seemed harmless enough. But suppose Gillian had chosen that moment to return to what after all is her favourite café. Suppose she had been overcome with an (admittedly uncharacteristic) bout of rudeness and curiosity and she had picked up our phone and tapped its screen so its light shone on her face. The next thing we know she has cleared her throat theatrically, giving every indication that she intends to speak. She looked confident and just a touch malicious at that point. She wanted the whole coffee shop to hear and it seemed to us that when the moment came her voice was almost deafening. Her shouting drowned out the sounds of banal community chatter, the Iberian off-stage bickering, the weedy mournful trumpet. It's not an exaggeration to say she screamed out what she saw there.

*WHAT ARE THE FULL LYRICS TO I DO LIKE TO BE BESIDE THE SEASIDE*

When we were little one of us thought it was wiggly.

## Panel Two: exactly why

The word—which he knew he knew perfectly well—remained just out of his reach. Unwanted? No. Unbidden? Well that worked but it wasn't the word he was trying to remember. Invasive? Seemed close. He decided to ask her.

What is that word for when you have thoughts in your head that you'd prefer weren't there but no matter what you do you can't stop thinking them? he said.

And I would know this exactly how? she said.

Intrusive, he said to an empty room.

When the thoughts first began he had tried to make light of the whole thing. He claimed it did little more than irk him. It was irksome, he would say, making use of an amusing term beloved of those types who make a virtue out of downplaying their emotions. Those silly merchants who pass off self-deprecation as personal culture. Until this new thing gripped him, he had enjoyed being one of those types. Impossible now when they recognised him but he couldn't tell them apart and there are words for what this brought out in him but none of them is irksome.

You see he knew that they didn't all look the same, clearly if they could pick him out of a crowd then they would have the means to distinguish between each other. The urge came on him to share his annoyance with somebody else, another one of his own kind. He needed to know if it was the same for everyone and if it bothered others as much as it bothered him.

Because it bothers me, he said.

I couldn't care less, she said.

They can tell us apart but to me and you they appear identical, he said again.

This affects my life how, she said and he cursed her phrasing.

You do realise that they are not identical, don't you? You have grasped that? To them they are as easily distinguishable as you and I are to each other. You do get that? Except they can also, apparently, distinguish between you and me with the same ease. See? Differences between each other, totally clear. Differences between you and me, no problem. Clear differences, clear, clear, clear, that we, idiot us, cannot see, he said.

And I'm supposed to care, why? she said and her syntax forced him to leave the room.

There's a field by the clifftop that overlooks the bay. He walked beside it once a week when he needed to chase unwelcome thoughts about his life from his head. But that strategy is doomed now because that field was always full of the bastards. Hundreds of them, all identical though apparently not. Of course, common sense and an article he had read online told them that this could not be.

The last time he walked along the clifftop by the field they looked at him, each of them, this legion of them, and they knew him. He focused on three that stood nearest to the path that separated the field from the cliffs. He considered their features closely as they considered his. The three made it as obvious as they could that they knew he was a different specimen to the woman who walked her dog up ahead or the young couple who squeezed past him with their pram. We know you and remember you, they implied, from last week at around this time. But also many other occasions.

He saw nothing. He checked their size and shape, searched for features around their bodies, heads and feet. Nothing. He examined their attitude, how they held themselves, their current mood. All identical. All the same, definitely. But he knew that they were not.

What they were, though, all of them, was relentless.

The day that followed that distressing walk saw a couple of them parade around his garden. Their curiosity was apparent in each inclination of their heads. First this way then that. They examined and explored the lawn, the plants along the borders and those in pots before they turned their attention to him.

They mocked, it seemed to him, his lack of savvy. They doubted—blatantly—his ability to survive should he be left to his own devices in extreme circumstances. What are you gonna do, they said, when your plane comes crashing down in the rainforest? What will you eat? How will you shelter? What are the essentials you will need to keep yourself safe? Or when your ship sinks just off the coast of a deserted island, what skills do you bring to the party of survivors? Who are you, they said, in this world that we get but you don't? What can you do? Look at us foraging here. Look at us making use of the scraps you have left lying around and building houses with them. See how we know you. See how we know her. Look at us fucking fly!

❋

And there was an office in a grey building on one of the industrial estates that surrounded the small town. He drove to it five days a week and sat at a desk from 8.30 till around 5pm, sometimes a little earlier and sometimes a little later depending on his day's workload. On that desk there were two computers, one of which showed columns of streaming numbers that appeared almost as soon as he switched it on. The other was for words. Next to the keyboard by the numbers computer he placed his home phone, the one he used to let her know if his workload meant he was going to be a little later or a little earlier than agreed before he left the house that morning. By the words keyboard sat another phone that was used for some communications allied to his workload. There, too, was a notepad and pen that he used for drawing pleasing geometric shapes whilst the numbers streamed past and the words flooded in.

Until recently his comfort with the words and numbers and the pleasing doodles had meant that the hours between 8.30 and approximately 5pm had, as they say, flown by. All had been well and good for many years, in fact, but lately, since the horrible problem of being recognised without being able to return that recognition had consumed him, though the numbers continued to flow and the word count rose and rose, he had found it difficult to concentrate. And his focus was showing no sign of a return. He still made geometric patterns with the pen on the notepad but they had ceased to be pleasing. He hardly noticed them now, nor did he bother to intervene with the information that piled up on the computer screens even though he must have, somewhere at the back of his mind, realised that this would lead to an increase, a backlog, in his workload that should have resulted in a stay at the office beyond his normal working hours. He didn't worry about a future text to her from the phone that sat next to the numbers computer that would apologise for how late he would be one night, that work had just piled up and up until there was no alternative but to sit there at his desk and knuckle down and clear that workload of numbers and words once and for all or at least until it all began again the next day. He wasn't worried about that at all. He was far too worried about the other two objects on his desk. All his attention was monopolised by these.

Behind the computer that collected the words for him to deal with there was a framed photograph of two smiling faces in extreme close up. The faces were the faces of two people well known to him. They were him and her. He couldn't remember who took this picture nor where it was taken. There were no clues he could see. No sky was visible nor any buildings. No clothing that may have let him in on what season it was. No reflections in the eyes of either him or her that might have shown, say, bright sunlight. There was nothing to help him.

And next to this photograph was a snow globe that showed a street scene with a church in its centre. This ornament had the word Riga attached to its front.

As far as he could remember he had never been to Riga and he could think of no friend, acquaintance or colleague that had ever mentioned the place.

Much of the time between 8.30 am and around about 5pm he stared at these objects and his hand that held the pen over the notebook made decidedly unpleasing shapes. These were now awful nightmarish scrawls that an observer prone to cliché might have said were a reflection on his state of mind.

He let the pen drop and turned off the computer screens. The numbers and words did not disappear, he knew, but he would not see them again till the next day. He managed to drag his attention away from the photograph and the snow globe and left the office on the industrial estate just outside the town.

On his drive home he swerved to avoid a dead dog lying in the middle of the road. When he had righted the car he looked in his rearview mirror and saw that it wasn't an animal, just a black bin bag. To calm himself down, to try to bring his heart within some acceptable beating boundary, he said, Don't fret, the black bag is not a dead dog. And that seemed to work.

✳

You're talking about what now, she said.

This photograph on my desk, he said.

And to be clear you want me to what? she said. Follow you to your office one morning before work and, like, examine some snapshot that you describe as what? Us two? Where are we? And I'd do this why?

To help me, he said. It's annoying me.

And you can't just bring it home to show me for what reason? she said.

BECAUSE I DIDN'T THINK. BECAUSE THINKING IS HARD NOW.

And shouting at me helps exactly how? she said.

✳

They sat on the fence at the side of the road, knowing him as he drove past. They knew everything but they were unknowable. Every single one of these bastards knew the difference between a dead dog and a bin bag.

He had resolved to bring home the framed photograph that showed a smiling couple in extreme close-up and that had sat next to his words computer for who knows how long. But he forgot. So he resolved to remember to do it the following evening but some forces seemed to be working against him and he forgot again. He acknowledged defeat and gave up. Whatever they were, these forces, they were stronger than him. Whatever their aims, they brought something— no word for what it was—out in him.

He sat at his desk in the office on the industrial estate and he couldn't see the numbers and words that flowed from the screens to his left and right and filled the room. He was ankle deep in workload and he was trying to think of what to call these feelings that the forces brought out in him. What do you call this feeling of helplessness that went hand in hand with a heightened awareness that his veins were a sci-fi subway system? It was one of the bad ones, he knew enough to know that. Anxiety. Despair. Anger. Depression. Fear. Panic. It was definitely one of the Top Six. And Inadequacy was there, lurking just outside the hit parade.

For now there was no such thing as a quiet sound nor any outlet for all of the light that poured into his eyes.

There were no faint scents.

Arms were nothing but broken wings.

He dreaded the idea of leaving that room and having to face questions from people he didn't know that needed answers that he didn't have.

What is it you do exactly?

When did you go to Riga?

Where was this taken?

Some words on the computer almost came into clear focus and he tried to take them in before they melted away then slithered down the screen before dripping off the table and forming part of the mass that lay at his feet.

Both computer screens stared back at him, sneering now and bereft of any information that could help him. They had both become stubbornly resistant to any form of interpretation. They defied understanding. What they knew they kept from him and they remained unknowable.

He looked down as the chaotic doodle he had made with the pen on the notebook. The opposite of pleasing is what. And my name is what, she said. He picked up the snow globe and shook it so that the street scene disappeared and, for the moment, ceased its torment. But when he waited for the snow to stop and the street to disappear, it never happened. It just kept falling until there was no such thing as gravity. So he placed it beside the supercilious numbers computer and picked up the framed photograph.

He peered at the two figures captured there.

They must have their own unique lives, their own different outlooks, their own private thoughts. Even there, smiling for an unknown photographer in an unknown place, they were trying to convey something to him. And his inability to grasp what that was must have frustrated them. Or made them mock him. He wanted to know what they wanted him to know but it was impossible.

As impossible as telling them apart.

### Panel Three: Dive, thoughts

I've bagsied us rather handsome digs, I say.

Smart chap you, you say, thank you.

You're welcome, darling, I say. I've certainly been in much worse.

I've heard all the tales before so let me stop you before you start, you say.

Do you remember the time when you went away somewhere and you were extremely unhappy with your accommodation? You called me up in absolute despair, asking me what should you do. I quickly reeled off five possible solutions to your problem and you were so grateful, immediately calmed. You went to fetch paper and pen so you could write down the five alternatives and asked me to repeat them. But I could only think of four. Weeks later I was still trying to recall the fifth but it never came to me.

Your mates woke me up early this morning. My God they make their presence felt, don't they? Screeching like they own the place.

They do own the place, you say.

So between them and the waves making that whooshwhoosh sound that old Krapp might relish, I've not had much kip. Not feeling what you might call refreshed for our big day.

The racket nature makes when it wants something.

Do you want to see me heave myself out from under the duvet and across to that bay window in one balletic movement? Of course you do. And once there you can watch me take a few moments to bend at the waist and cough up my lungs.

See me standing there in my vest and underpants with one bollock, typically, making a run for it.

See me survey the scene like a tuxedoed spy, scanning the casino for opportunity and threat.

A horseshoe bay, I say, expanding from the harbour arm to the tidal pool. There are kids there with little fishing nets sifting for crabs. Vile creatures, you say, and I know you don't mean the crabs. The sea seems a little less Wagner and a little more Debussy now. There are trampolines. Dogs of both the wet and the fearful variety. Overweight hearty swimmers strain the possibilities of their wetsuits. A giant inflatable, it goes without saying, giraffe. Licensed chippy, licensed caff trapped behind the beach huts, harbour bar, a pub-like airport bar, beach bar, pub like a pub. Four places for ice cream. Four places for chips.

What else? you say.

Sand. And sky. Yellow. And blue, I say.

Like the Ukrainian flag, you say.

The things you know, I say.

I've been looking at your books, I say. Books in boxes, on windowsills, piled up next to the bed, the settee. I decided to set aside those that were memoirs by women writers, don't ask why, and I have been working my way through them these past weeks. Enjoyable stuff, for the most part, though I have my doubts about whether your ladies always tell me the truth. Of course, they can never have an opinion about me and whether I can be trusted so, in a way, I have all the advantages in my relationship with your favourite writers. I hold all the cards. I'm winning.

Shall we get down amongst it? Get showered and dressed and maybe have a coffee and croissant in the unfriendly shade of those gruesome beach huts?

Do you remember that gig I had touring the Baltic states with some farce? I was drinking so much in those days that I was always forgetting to buy you a present. Hence that odd collection of tourist souvenirs from airport gift shops that takes up a boxful of space in our loft. Well my thoughtless gift to you from Riga mysteriously appeared on the Reception desk downstairs, or an exact replica of it at least. I meant to tell you last night after we checked in but sleep must have overtaken me.

No need for socks today. A boon.

Do you remember when those weird ghoulish Canadian chaps tracked you down because you had the same surname as them? One of those internet atrocities, I suspect. They came in for a cup of tea and they asked you if you had any family pictures you could show them. I have no effing time for c-word nostalgia, you said. Glorious.

I must stop asking you do you remember.

The rule is that you are allowed to curse but I am not. Thank you for that, a tiresome excess avoided. You have so much more self-control.

Ah. Two of your friends are here to greet you. Should I describe them? Well they are sitting side by side and all their attention is, naturally, focused on you. I realise I am surplus to requirements in this particular encounter. The one on the left, our left, is long and supermodel sleek. She really is gorgeous. But shy, not quite timid, but less forthcoming than her partner. He is a cocky brute, absolutely full of himself, built like a Victorian bare knuckle scoundrel and eyeing you up like a new parlour maid.

There they go. Up and up. We have served our purpose. Which you know but won't tell me, you tease.

Shall we walk up and down the beach? Do I dare to eat a peach?

Eliot wrote part of *The Waste Land* near here, you say.

The things you know, I say.

What about that *Murder In The Cathedral* in the spooky old church in Suffolk? I say. Me growling along as the Fourth Knight. God you have had to sit through some dross, haven't you, darling? Clarence in Clwyd. I'd cringe but that was by no means the worst.

Some buffoon has left a large black plastic bag on the sand. I think I would pick it up anyway but your being with me means I have no choice. I pull up the wretched thing, sopping, gritty, and look around for a waste bin.

One of those wiry dogs runs out of the water and shakes itself near us so I can feel the droplets on my bare ankles.

I can feel the sun beating down on my bald patch like the malevolent god he has always been.

They're all malevolent, you say. All shits.

Once . . . though I choose not to remind you of this, not in your current mood . . . once I played God in the Mystery Plays at Chester. He was a kindly soul with a drink problem, as I remember.

Are you doing OK? Is this the right place?

Sometimes you do not answer and I understand.

I can see what attracts you to this place, I say, why you wished to be brought here. The sort of good old fashioned fun that appeals to your democratic soul, it's a great leveller, isn't it, the seaside? Kids are equal to, or able to escape from, their owners. Pets . . . so-called pets, you would have it . . . are able to play at being wild animals. And the actual wild animals are not skulking about, hiding behind any available flora waiting for us to leave. They're ruling the joint, allowing us a little fun on their territory. I can see why you approve. We exist here for their pleasures and needs, Tudor courtiers living it up at the grace and favour of the monarch but surely with the same niggling thought at the back of all our minds. Our life expectancy is not of our choosing; we're all for the chop.

Yes, you say. I love that. I love the very idea of that.

Your friends circle around above us, crying to each other. It is a crying beyond my ken and one that you choose not to explain. I am reminded of a misjudged Captain Hook in Coventry many years ago, my villainy reducing the toddlers to hysterical tears in the afternoon dark.

More appear just above our heads and fly in sympathetic circle. They are whooping like Vikings at a warrior's funeral.

I love that sound, you say.

And my aches and pains have gone for a little break, too, I say.

That's good, dear, you say.

I take a stage breath. An old king on the moor

And my lungs feel filled with something nutritious, I say.

Ozone, you say.

The things you know, I say.

Crying for all of us.

I cast an eye around the careless crowd.

I could ruin it for them, of course, I say. I could spoil their hols if I wanted to. I could plant m feet wide apart and stand four square and centr stage and face the waves and rail at the sea in m ridiculous booming voice. I could summon u some mishmash of Titus A and what I can re member from that dementia patient in Holb City. I could scare them to death. If you like . . .

No, dear, you say. It's a lovely thought, but n thank you.

Circling like critics, understanding before th rest of the audience gets it that I am in need of prompt.

You've gone very quiet, you say.

Just a little lost, I say. Just trying to decide o the spot.

I know, you say.

Where to leave you, I say.

I know, you say. It'll come to you.

I don't know how to leave you, I say.

Like falling off an effing log, you say.

I don't . . . I say.

Like riding a c-word bike, you say.

Cries of impatience from your friends above They, like you, want this to be over with.

I want you to choose, I say.

That's just you being silly, dear, you say.

I want you to choose, I say.

NICK HOLDSTOCK

# PARTIAL OBJECT

My Very Dearest Deborah,

I've made a table for you. Your table is in your bedroom. Before you enter I would like you to pause, take several slow breaths, put down the hammer, and allow me to explain.

No doubt you are wondering, *Why another table when I already have three*? A spice rack or extra stool would have made more sense. These would be practical. These would meet a lack.

But this is a table we need. I didn't like the way we left things when you went to the airport. I didn't like being called 'spineless'. I didn't like that I kept silent. After you slammed the door I stayed here, even though I know you hate me being at your place without you. I was waiting for the impossible, hoping you'd decide I was more important than a bunch of Brueghels. I confess I stayed the night, but only on the couch. Next morning, when you still hadn't called, let alone returned, I understood that our problems could not be remedied by talking. I realised that only something tangible could bridge the gap between us. Ideally, I'd have gone to the hardware store for nails and wood—and also picked up some groceries—but because you've never given me a key, I have had to stay here for the last five days. I have had to improvise.

The first thing you'll notice about your table is that it has seven legs, because I wanted it to be lucky, and I wanted it to be steady. I admit I have wobbled. When you lose your temper, I run. Instead of accepting the force of the storm, the hurled glasses and plates, I seek shelter in a library, a bar, the number 37 bus whose route is a rough circle. For this I am sorry. In the future I will be as loyal as furniture. My two legs shall be as still and steady as those lucky seven. If there was time, and more wood in your flat, I would have added more. Ten, eleven, fifteen legs would really make my point. But as you often remind me, I have limitations. I am neither tall nor handsome. I dress for comfort. I cannot create

wood from nothing. I had to borrow the legs of your bed, the curtain rails from the lounge and bedroom, the base of the lamp in the hall. You never used that hockey stick. Bookcases are cheap.

Pascal was of the opinion that there was once, in man, a true happiness, of which all that now remains is an infinite abyss that can be filled only with an infinite and immutable object. Pascal really liked God. In our relationship there is a similar void (though obviously far smaller than the absence of the deity). I love you and I am certain you love me even though you've never said so. You will not say, 'Moi aussi.' You cannot even say 'Likewise.' Yet I don't doubt that you feel something stronger than tolerance. We see each other twice a week; it's been almost a year. Never mind where our relationship is going; think of where it has been.

I spent a lot of time trying to decide the form of the table. The L-shape was a late inspiration that arrived at the end of the second day. As I sat on the lounge carpet, eating spaghetti with hot dog mustard, I flipped through my memories of our dinners, hoping to find an image of you smiling as you spooned my raspberry panna cotta, my crème brûlée, my white chocolate roulade. Once I'd finished crying (I couldn't find a single instance) I realised that the attempt betrayed my real motives for making those elaborate desserts. Instead of being satisfied with the knowledge that I had made a lovely pudding, and that you like lovely puddings, I stared at your face like a dog desperate for scraps. I have to learn to accept that your love for me is not an infinite and immutable object. I have to let you eat. And so when you return we shall sit at right angles from each other. Having you in my periphery needs to be enough.

Of course you are wondering about the holes. The biggest hole represents Jeremy, the middle-sized one is Tristan, the smallest hole is for something else. I can no longer pretend those two princes did not exist. I thought the benevolent smoke of my love could act as a curtain that would shroud your past, help you forget, but when you shouted, 'You fucking snake' at me you were addressing one of those villains. Tristan, who flew you to Florence and Paris and was knowledgeable about wine, antiques, how shoes were made, where to moor a yacht. Tristan who was a coward without self-control. I'm sure he thought his infidelities trivial, a waitress here, a cultural attaché there, little accidents that could

spent most of your time with that picture trying to fathom its glazes. You wanted to know how many layers of varnish had been required. You suspected Tintoretto had used a badger brush to make the colours lie. The green was thus not really green. The green was 'Yellow Lake' varnish

not divert the straight course of your love. And it is entirely understandable that you said nothing for months. You were not sure. They were only suspicions. Otherwise you were happy. Yes, you were checking his phone, his pockets, his browser history, but as far as you knew you were looking for clues to a mystery that didn't exist.

And then you found his second phone. He cried. He begged. I'm sure his remorse was convincing. And you definitely did not make it easy for him. For the three weeks you travelled with him you slept in separate rooms. Every time a pretty stewardess or waitress deployed some professional charm you reminded Tristan of what he'd done. I am sure that his apologies, in furniture terms, were an entire dining set. And he was not stupid. He knew what arranging a private viewing of Tintoretto's *Diana and Endymion* would mean to you. You told me you

spread over a patch of 'Cobalt Blue'. But you could not be sure without an X-ray, and the owners would not allow that. You took this personally. Two years later, when you told me this story, you broke a wine glass. You said people had a right to know.

But you also said those six hours alone with the painting were still like looking through a window that showed myth. You marvelled at its luminosity. For a brief time there was no sense of separation between you and the painting. You saw the image from within the painting. And so you took him back.

You say you were happy for the next six months. You say you did not check his phone or question his frequent absences. This was not stupid. You were not blind. You thought you deserved to be happy, and if this included flying business class to walk on white sand with only turtles for company, there was nothing wrong with that. You shouldn't be ashamed of your optimism. Giving him a second chance was an act of faith few are capable of. What I ask now, what this table intends, is that you should allow us that reprieve.

(By the way—you'll need bigger plates. Your current ones fall through the holes.)

As for Jeremy, that was not your fault. You were just unlucky. In no way should his superficial similarity to Tristan have been a warning sign. They were different chairs. Tristan had blonde hair; Jeremy had brown. Tristan had no ear for music; Jeremy could play Saint-Saen's *Rondo Capriccioso*. And Tristan, for all his failings, was not a monster. I'm sure that if he heard a story in which some other man did what he'd done to you he'd be appalled. Only a monster would view that story of suffering and near-insanity as an opportunity. Though I am not a violent man, I confess I would like to use these rudimentary carpentry tools on Jeremy. Though it was awful for him to have an affair with your Teaching Assistant, his response to being accused was as different from Tristan's as a four-poster bed is to a cot. For him to suggest that your suspicions about his unexplained absences were the result of your chronic inability to trust was like pushing you off a cliff. And so the affair went on. The gaslighting continued. He even dared to suggest that your issues had forced Tristan to sleep with the waitresses. Those mind games would have messed anyone up. No wonder you started drinking. Your colleagues are just as much to blame for not correcting you when, during your lectures, you kept saying 'Vermin' instead of 'Vermeer'.

And I am to blame for being naive enough to believe that by gifting you a small parcel of affection every day for the last ten months—bringing it like the cup of Darjeeling with which you start every morning—I might eventually convince you that I can be trusted. Once again, I am sorry. Those holes that represent Jeremy and Tristan will stop me from underestimating the scale of the challenge you face every day. I'm glad I slashed my arm while cutting them out. The scar will remind me that what those men did will follow you as doggedly as that mahogany escritoire you bought in Hong Kong, shipped to Berlin, then New York, then here. I hesitated for such a long time before using its drawers. I hope I wasn't wrong to use their hardwood in the service of our future.

In the cold light of this cold morning—your heating system baffles me—when you will be home in two hours, I must confess that the table's third hole is probably a mistake. At four a.m. it made perfect sense. Now I've no idea what I was thinking. Something about wholeness and the implicate order; something about Saint Ignatius. The best I can say is that the hole is a nod to incompleteness. I am just an odd-shaped man. No table can fix you. This is simply love as furniture and love is not always enough.

So maybe you will raise the hammer I wrapped this note around. In only four or five blows you can reduce your table to shards. It is not a strong construction; the more I worked on your table, the flimsier it became. But let me offer this warning: the varnish will certainly be wet. The first two coats, being thinner, dried quickly, but this last, thicker treatment, will require more time. And it's better to smash a dry table than a sticky one. Better to wait a little. Then at least you'll see the true colour of your table. The grenadine I added to the first two layers made a rich, bright red. But the last layer, which has nothing added, will be completely transparent. Once dry, it will act as a lens that focuses the morning sun onto the table's surface. I hope that saturated red will seem to pulse and beat.

Terena Elizabeth Bell

# Alice, You've Got to Face It You've Been Holding this Back for Years

Alice had acted out—not at dinner, holding her temper in the restaurant, the car—but the minute they got home she told Allen, "I'm unhappy," because she was. She was miserable. She was so absolutely miserable she wanted him to see it, her soon-to-be crying face, but when Allen did look, when he finally did look at her, all he said was "You're not the only one in this marriage with regrets, you know."

She was trying—or had been trying at least—but it got old. It had gotten old and had been old for a very long time and she walked toward the bedroom to pack. She'd file for separation, live on her own, slamming her Samsonite suitcase on the bed.

Next to the master bath, where she scooped up elixirs and creams, moisturizers and lotions, throwing them in a bag. She ran her arm along the top of the counter to slide in the makeup and that's when Alice saw it: the bathrobe he'd given her senior year. It was a rat ass thing. It was a rat ass, belabored old thing and Allen himself had said "throw it out" many times. It was the last thing he'd bought her before she found out she was pregnant and that this had meant grad school would not be in store, the robe she put on when she lost the child. It was the most comforting thing she owned, if only because it reminded her of how she'd wanted things to be.

She stood there. Alice stood in the bathroom, suitcase on the bed outside, and lowered the bag to cry.

Allen was right. At dinner, when he'd said she should just give up, give up and admit it was too late to do most of what she'd wanted back when they were young, that life had passed her by. He wasn't even thinking when he said it, eyes on the menu, entree descriptions and a wine list, never looking at her face.

Then, at the door, a click. She didn't know what she would tell him when he saw the suitcase, saw her standing in the bathroom with a Lancome bag full of things. Maybe she'd get lucky and the cocktails from dinner would kick in and Allen wouldn't even notice. Maybe he wouldn't come in. Maybe he'd do that thing he does where he goes in the living room and takes off his shoes and throws his feet on the coffee table and acts like she isn't here—not because he didn't want her, but because maybe sometimes he wanted to feel like he was still 21 with promise too.

Quietly, oh so quietly, Alice took out the foundation. She placed it back on the bathroom counter, then the mascara, the concealer, the blush—anything she could grab without making noise—one beauty item at a time. One bottle, one tube, one everything in succession until she felt secure enough to walk in the bedroom. The bag wasn't empty—women had too much stuff—but the suitcase was still out and she needed to put it away and if she didn't in time, well, she could tell Allen she'd taken it down for cleaning. "These old Samsonites, Allen," she would say, "you know sometimes they get that weird powdery gunk that comes out from under the lining. I really should just throw it away."

Fortunately she didn't have to say anything as she heard him go not toward the bedroom, but the kitchen instead. "Alice," Allen yelled, "honey, you want a drink?" and "I'm going for a walk," Alice shouted.

"This late?"

"Yeah," she said. "I love you."

Marvin Cohen

# From Marvin's Shoebox

### His Reading Taste a Matter of What He Likes, How He Rectifies a Reading Mistake, By Eradicating What He's Just Read When He Realizes Too Late That He's Not Liked It.

D o you like spy stories?

No.

Why?

Because I don't read them. I only like what I read.

But what if you read something and you *don't* like it?

Then I stop reading it.

But what if you don't stop *quick* enough?

Then when I *do* stop, I carefully undo all the reading I've just done, by reading that passage backwards, till it slides right out of my system. Then I'm cleansed of it; and look forward to some *good* reading, next time.

## A Monologue on the Dialogue

I recommend the dialogue as a way of dramatizing our two constant inward voices that are always either agreeing or disputing or qualifying each other or something: the "out-there" representation in the self, and the "in-here" assertions of the self. We "take on" an "other-people, outside-world" view, to toughly challenge or confirm our "more personal" subjectivity. Thus, dialogues are always rolling in us. We should externalize them by writing them. The polarity-opposition-tension of a dialogue form may ring out a more universal fiber to the reader than the too-temptingly-soft, all-first-person, one-way writings that go unchecked, unbalanced, unanswered, by an opposing stance, tone, or key.

Another good thing about the dialogue form is that it gives an alternative opportunity in between writing a whole damn stiff formal play (with names, characterizations, descriptions, plot, development) on the one hand, and writing nothing in any dramatic vein on the other.

Any person attempting to do something in the dialogue form gets the following encouragement from me: "Good luck to both of you."

## A Truth Ill-fitted in a Cliché

Once, a truth was born. To celebrate, its parents bought it a suitable verbal outfit. But the truth's nakedness was garbed in a cliché! The truth bawled and squealed, protesting the unsuitable outward form. It was strait-jacketed by such a suit of cliche! The truth's integrity felt violated, down to its marrow. It detested being seen in attire stitched of so commonplace a fabric, along lines so detestably familiar to any stupid passerby! It craved to wear robes of esoteric ambiguity, to stun the onlooker with its depth of mystery! But the truth was doomed: every fool recognizes it as a cliché. Its apparel betrays its unique origin. Vested in a cliché, the truth has lost its original quality, and walks down the boulevard in a dreary pedestrian procession. What a mundane fate, for a truth born with such great promise! The dead outer flesh of a worn cliché!

## The Book I Read—It's Being Freshly Authored By Me. I'm Redoing It, The Original Script Is Unrecognizable, By Now. It's Become Incorporated By The World As I'm Writing It.

Since touching that book, I've carried it around mentally. It's being rewritten by me. The author's original words are being constantly revised, until the book has become—is—will become—my very creation. I acknowledge indebtedness, and credit my source. But the author pales, his original work fades. My reconstruction is the living vital tissue now, with blood-veins and a crosswork of nerves, with fiber, marrow, gristle, skin, clothing, hair, personality, presence. Organically, it's become me. Thank you, old author. It's beyond recognition by you now. I ripped it away, and transformed my appropriation, grafted the confiscation into a new surgical embodiment. The book has a new soul—my own. I steal nature from itself. Trees and stones are stripped away—people too; welcome to my world imperialism. I claim whatever I bite off. I chew on the city, the countryside. They enter in with what that book became. My expanding universe.

Sean Ennis

# Three Disorders

## Desire Disorder

How to say this without hurting feelings? I've gotten smarter and I'm bored. I'm a stuffed complaint box. Different types of people hate me. This school administrator with a desire disorder. This color-blind software developer. My wife of twenty years, my son of sixteen. Even that customer service chatbot that caught me in its loop. I was on the airplane when the passenger pointed out that that motherfucker back there isn't real. Laugh if you want. I've sat by that motherfucker too—that rich woman is a hero. When we debriefed in the airport lounge, I hadn't had a drink in a decade. She was complaining for her refund and was deep in the customer service chat. The war she had started was already over. I missed my flight. Solipsism syndrome has a treatment if you frame it that way.

## Now Suffer

At first, I felt psychosexual at dinner, I think, like a crime-fighting surfer or a monk in love with a nun. Am I using this word right? I felt invigorated and confused. This was our first date. Rita complained about the professionalization of the game show Jeopardy and men faking orgasms. I was unprepared for this—there's nothing helpful in my notes—but I felt to be in the presence of a confounding worldview. I chewed and chewed on my bread. Later, she brutalized me in her bedroom, and then gave me a Dixie cup of water and some orange slices. The sun was coming up when I prayed to my late wife. I didn't tell her everything, but she knew. I evacuated my memories. It was safer that way. Prayer is not a conversation.

## Focalisation

We ran through our mutual, amateur interest in particle acceleration results and early Christian anchorites, and then, what is there left to say? Boy, we could use some rain? The last article I read about the LHC said they discovered the gluon responsible for lust and St. Simeon thought the best way to live was on top of a twenty-foot pole. Demons afflicted Syncletica with a mouth infection so bad that the smell repelled visitors. A neutrino was discovered in Antarctica that can be traced to the rapidly spinning blazar at the center of a distant galaxy. However, I got yelled at at work? My favorite sports team won't make the playoffs? My wife? Yes, it's hot in Mississippi in August, we could linger on that. But, how incredible that our interests did converge! We stopped talking in a friendly way.

# Uranium Chant

I.

Uranium Anium Anium Anium
Uranium Anium Anium Anium
Uranium Anium Anium Anium
Uranium Anium Anium Anium

Anium Anium Uranium Anium
Anium Anium Uranium Anium
Anium Anium Uranium Anium
Anium Anium Uranium Anium

Anium Anium Uranium, Yum! Yum! Yum!
Anium Anium Uranium, Yum! Yum!
Uranium Anium Anium , Yum! Yum! Yum!
Uranium Anium Anium , Yum! Yum!

Anium Anium Uranium, Yum! Yum! Yum!
Anium Anium Uranium, Yum! Yum!
Uranium Anium Anium , Yum! Yum! Yum!
Uranium Anium Anium , Yum! Yum!

Uranium Anium Anium Anium
Uranium Anium Anium Anium
Uranium Anium Anium Anium
Uranium, Uranium, Uranium, Uranium, Uranium Anium Anium Anium!

Uranium Anium Anium Anium
Anium Anium Uranium Anium!
Uranium Anium Anium Anium

Uranium, Yum! Yum! Uranium Yum! Uranium Yum! Yum! Yum!
Uranium Yum!  Uranium Anium Anium Anium

Uranium, Yum! Yum! Uranium Yum!  Uranium Yum! Yum! Yum!
Uranium Yum!  Uranium Anium Anium Anium

Anium Anium, Yum!Yum!
Anium Anium, Yum!Yum!
Anium Anium Yum! Yum!
Anium Anium Yum! Yum!

Anium Anium Anium Anium
Anium Anium Anium Anium
Yum! Yum!  Yum! Yum!
Yum! Yum!  Yum! Yum!

Yumanium  Yumanium  Yumanium  Yumanium
Yumanium  Yumanium  Yumanium  Yumanium

MANIYAyayayayayayayayayaya ....................!
MANIYAyayayayayayayayayaya ....................!

*MANIYA-YA-YA-YA-YA-YA-YAH!!!*           *(Fine)*

## II.

Urine Urine Urine,Urine Urine Urine,Urine Urine Urine,Urine Urine Urine
Urine Urine Urine,Urine Urine Urine,Urine Urine Urine,Urine Urine Urine

Urine Urine Urine, Urine Urine Ur/Inure Inure Inure, Inure Inure Inure
Urine Urine Urine, Urine Urine Ur/Inure Inure Inure, Inure Inure Inure

Urine Urine Urine, Urine Urine Urine /Inner Inner Inner, Inner Inner Inner
Urine Urine Urine, Urine Urine Urine /Inner Inner Inner, Inner Inner Inner
Urine Urine Urine, Urine Urine Urine /Inner Inner Inner, Inner Inner Inner

Urine Inure Inner, Urine Inure Inner, Urine Inure Inner,
Urine Inure Inner, Urine Inure Inner, Urine Inure Inner,

Urine Inner Inure, Urine Inner Inure, Urine Inner Inure,
Urine Inner Inure, Urine Inner Inure, Urine Inner Inure,

Inure Inure Inure, Inure Inure Inure
Inure Inure Inure, Inure Inure Inure

Injure Injure Injure, Injure Injure Injure,
Urine Urine Urine, Urine Urine Urine
Injure Injure Injure, Injure Injure Injure,
Inure Inure Inure, Inure Inure Inure
Injure Injure Injure, Injure Injure Injure,
Inner Inner Inner, Inner Inner Inner
Injure Injure Injure, Injure Injure Injure,
Urine Inure Inner, Urine Inure Inner, Urine Inure Inner,
Urine Inure Inner, Urine Inure Inner, Urine Inure Inner,

Inure Inure Inure, Inure Inure Inure,
Urine Inure Inner, Urine Inure Inner, Urine Inure Inner,
Urine Inure Inner, Urine Inure Inner, Urine Inure Inner
Urine Inner Inure, Urine Inner Inure, Urine Inner Inure,
Urine Inner Inure, Urine Inner Inure, Urine Inner Inure,

Inure Inure Inure, Inure Inure Inure
Inure Inure Inure, Inure Inure Inure

Injure Anium, Injure Anium, Injure Anium Anium Anium
Urine Urine Urine, Urine Urine Urine
Injure Anium, Injure Anium, Injure Anium Anium Anium
Urine Inure Urine Inure Urine Inure Urine Inure
Injure Anium, Injure Anium, Injure Anium Anium Anium
Inner Inner Inner Inner, Inner Inner Inner Inner
Injure Anium, Injure Anium, Injure Anium Anium Anium
Urine Inner Inure, Urine Inner Inure, Urine Inner Inure, Urine Inner Inure
Inner Inure, Inner Inure,Inner Inure, Inner Inure,Inner Inure, Inner Inure,
Inure. Inure. Inure. Inure. Inure. Inure .............
*(SLOW)* Geranium, Geranium, Geranium, Geranium ...............
Anium, Anium, Anium, Anium .......................................................

# III.

**Yum!**
**YUMMY!**
**Yum!**
**YUMMY!**
**Yum!**
**YUMMY! YUMMY! YUMMY!**

**Yum!**
**YUMMY!**
**Yum!**
**YUMMY!**
**Yum!**
**YUMMY! YUMMY! YUMMY!**

*(Slow Growing in Intensity)*

**Yummy! Yummy! Yummy! Yummy!**
**Yummy! Yummy! Yummy! Yummy!**
**Yummy! Yummy! Yummy! Yummy!**
**Yummy! Yummy! Yummy! Yummy!**

*(Suddenly Rapid, Soft , Metrical)*

**Yummy Jhana Yummy Jhana Jhana Yummy Jhana**
**Yummy Jhana Yummy Jhana Jhana Yummy Jhana**
**Yummy Jhana Yummy Jhana Jhana Yummy Jhana**
**Yummy Jhana Yummy Jhana Jhana Yummy Jhana**

**Yummy Jhana Yummy Jhana Jhana Jhana Yummy Jhana**
**Yummy Jhana Yummy Jhana Jhana Jhana Yummy Jhana**
**Yummy Jhana Yummy Jhana Jhana Jhana Yummy Jhana**
**Yummy Jhana Yummy Jhana Jhana Jhana Yummy Jhana**

**Yum Jhana Yum Jhana Yum Jhana Jhana**
**Yum Jhana Yum Jhana Yum Jhana Jhana**
**Yum Jhana Yum Jhana Yum Jhana Jhana**

**Yum Jhana Yum Jhana Yum Jhana Jhana Jhana**
**Yum Jhana Yum Jhana Yum Jhana Jhana Jhana**
**Yum Jhana Yum Jhana Yum Jhana Jhana Jhana**

**In Geranium! Jhana Uranium! In Geranium! Jhana Uranium!**
**Jhana Uranium! In Geranium! Jhana Jhana Jhana Uranium!**
**In Geranium! Jhana Uranium! In Geranium! Jhana Uranium!**
**Jhana Uranium! In Geranium! Jhana Jhana Jhana Uranium!**

Yum! Uranium, Yum! Uranium,
Yummy, Yum! Uranium! Yum! Uranium
Yummy, Yum! Uranium! , Yum! Uranium
Yummy, Yum! Uranium! , Yum! Uranium
Yummy, Yum! Uranium! , Yum! Uranium

Yum! Jhana Yummy! Jhana Yum! Uranium Anium Anium
Yummy Jhana Jhana Yummy Yum! Uranium Anium Anium
Yum! Jhana Yummy! Jhana Yum! Uranium Anium Anium
Yummy Jhana Jhana Yummy Yum! Uranium Anium Anium

GeRAYnium, GeRAYnium, GeRAYnium, GeRAYnium ...............
Uranium Uranium, Uranium Uranium Uranium .................
Anium Anium Anium Anium ........................................

## IV

Atom Atom Atom, Atom Atom Atom, Atom Atom  Atom, Atom Atom  Atom,
Atom Atom Atom, Atom Atom  Atom, Atom Atom  Atom, Atom Atom  Atom,
Mata Mata Mata,Mata Mata Mata,Mata Mata Mata,Mata Mata Mata
Mata Mata Mata,Mata Mata Mata,Mata Mata Mata,Mata Mata Mata

Atom Atom Atom, Atom Atom Atom, Atom Atom  Atom, Atom Atom  Atom,
Mata Mata Mata,Mata Mata Mata,Mata Mata Mata,Mata Mata Mata
Atom Atom Atom, Atom Atom Atom, Atom Atom  Atom, Atom Atom  Atom,
Mata Mata Mata,Mata Mata Mata,Mata Mata Mata,Mata Mata Mata

I Meta Meta I Meta, I Mata Mata I Mata
I Meta Meta I Meta, I Mata Mata I Mata
I Meta Meta I Meta, I Mata Mata I Mata
I Meta Meta I Meta, I Mata Mata I Mata

I Meta Tomato, I Meta I Meta Tomato, I Meta Meta I Meta Tomato
I Meta Tomato, I Meta I Meta Tomato, I Meta Meta I Meta Tomato
I Meta Tomato, I Meta I Meta Tomato, I Meta Meta I Meta Tomato

I Meta Physicist, I Meta I Meta Physicist, I Meta Meta I Meta Physicist
I Meta Physicist, I Meta I Meta Physicist, I Meta Meta I Meta Physicist
I Meta Physicist, I Meta I Meta Physicist, I Meta Meta I Meta Physicist

### *I MET A URANIUM ATOM!*

I Met A Uranium Atom, I Met A Uranium Atom, I Met A Uranium Atom,
I Met A Uranium Atom, I Met A Uranium Atom, I Met A Uranium Atom,

Atom Atom Atom, Atom Atom Atom, Atom Atom  Atom, Atom Atom  Atom,
Atom Atom Atom, Atom Atom Atom, Atom Atom  Atom, Atom Atom  Atom,
Mata Mata Mata, Mata Mata Mata, Mata Mata Mata, Mata Mata Mata
Mata Mata Mata, Mata Mata Mata, Mata Mata Mata,  Mata Mata Mata

Atom Meta, Atom Meta,  Atom Meta Meta
Atom Meta, Atom Meta,  Atom Meta Meta
Atom Meta, Atom Meta,  Atom Meta Meta
Atom Meta, Atom Meta,  Atom Meta Meta

I Meta Republican, I Meta I Meta Republican, I Meta Meta I Meta Republican
I Meta Republican, I Meta I Meta Republican, I Meta Meta I Meta Republican
I Meta Republican, I Meta I Meta Republican, I Meta Meta I Meta Republican

I Metan Autocrat, I Meta I Metan Autocrat, I Meta Meta I Metan Autocrat
I Metan Autocrat, I Meta I Metan Autocrat, I Meta Meta I Metan Autocrat
I Metan Autocrat, I Meta I Metan Autocrat, I Meta Meta I Metan Autocrat

I Meta Plutocrat, I Meta I Meta Plutocrat, I Meta Meta I Meta Plutocrat
I Meta Plutocrat, I Meta I Meta Plutocrat, I Meta Meta I Meta Plutocrat
I Meta Plutocrat, I Meta I Meta Plutocrat, I Meta Meta I Meta Plutocrat

## I MET A PLUTONIUM ATOM!

I Met A Plutonium Atom, I Met A Plutonium Atom, I Met A Plutonium Atom,
I Met A Plutonium Atom, I Met A Plutonium Atom, I Met A Plutonium Atom,

Plutonium Onium Onium Onium   Plutonium Onium Onium Onium
Plutonium Onium Onium Onium   Onium Onium Plutonium Onium
Plutonium Onium Onium Onium   Plutonium Onium Onium Onium
Plutonium Onium Onium Onium   Onium Onium Plutonium Onium

Plutonium Onium Onium Onium   Onium Onium Plutonium Onium
Plutonium Onium Onium Onium   Onium Onium Plutonium Onium

Anium Onium Anium Onium Anium Onium Anium Onium
AniINium AniONium AniONium AniONium ................
Onium Onium Onium Onium .................

Atom Meta, Atom Meta, Atom Meta Meta, Atom Meta, Atom Meta Meta
Atom Meta, Atom Meta, Atom Meta Meta, Atom Meta, Atom Meta Meta

Yum! Jhana Yummy! Jhana Yum! Uranium Anium Anium
Yummy Jhana Jhana Yummy Yum! Uranium Anium Anium

*(Very Slow, Crescendo)*

Yum! Yummy Yummy  Yummy Yummy Yummy Yummy ......
Yum! Yummy Yummy  Yummy Yummy Yummy Yummy ......
Yum! Yummy Yummy  Yummy Yummy Yummy Yummy ......

OM OM OM OM
OM OM OM OM
OM OM OM OM ...............................          *(DaCapo al Fine)*

Oisín Breen

# Four Poems

## The Quickening of the Black Gall

Our warders' hands are brass plated steel,
And their death comes in three states, each a chrysalis:
Before, now, and after; and each is pregnant with birth.
And in each state, they yearn to satisfy their thirst.

They yearn for ripe flesh, too, and fat tongues,
And for that state of being rarely touched and rarely known:

     a cathartic, stimulating gall,
     a gushing out of human meat,
     willed from want:
     a wanted infestation
     of fever(ing) for another,

     a kalanchoe, whose stems grow
     dark green wormskin,
     and a thick white matted fur,
     in whorls that wrap together,
     so sustaining the poison in the wound
     it becomes the remedy,
     rotten with satiety.

And they taste it, that black gall,
That shared gall of the muck,
And they want it all the more.

# The Ritual

A melody bleeds inside my bones,
It is my volcanic prayer of want.

    I know what it is to want,
    I know what it is I want:

This is my volcanic prayer

    of jagged lines,
    of starlight shifting beneath my bones,
    of hands moving, of hands touching,
    of racing hands, of learning hands,
    of eyes drinking, of eyes being drank,
    of the charcoal dark that covers my hips from sight,
    of the changing of the light,
    of showing my hips in the light,
    of a rising feeling beneath my hips in the shadow-night,
    of sharing myself with you in the shadow-light.

This is my volcanic prayer—

And each night, when the pendulum of star-light drops,
Each night, for months, when the tide-locked bell sounds its loudest,
Each night, since I first came here, when the sun sets,
I retreat to my cabin old and once remade,
To know best this choreography of skin.
To share it with you.
It is my loving prayer.

# Memories of the Grass and Clouds

I remember feeling what it is to be the multitude,
The sum of all the forms past—

And I remember how sweet it is
To feel the air and light dance upon my blades,
As young beetles skitter in skirls up my wind-longing
Deep-hanging summer heights.

I remember how sweet it is here
In fields no scythe has reaped,
As the worms tend that admixture of chemicals,
In which I first shed my seed-skin:

    its, a security of darkness,
    before the cherished touch of sun.

I remember, too, how complete it is to linger,
When I am a rhapsody of captured heat,
Even though I have seen lightning char
The water in which I swim,
Even though I have seen a reservoir
Soar as high as great and ancient birds,
And I felt, too, the black powder burn,
And nitrate turn slag light
Sending heavy metals soaring,
And I want only to return:

    rainfall
    from cloud to sea—

# A Journey on a Sligo Bus

The carriage came,
And its livery was red and white:
A lacquer flame.
And its patterning,
Likely once a dream of haste,
Sang of distance and regret.

And as the door swung open,
Sliding first out then back against the carriage bulk,
I, the only one to wait, stepped on
Eager to ease the hard body burden
    of the evening's trek.

And I gave my tiredness over to the watch
    of pistons, gears, and spirit steel.

And I gave my body over to rest;
    to foam seats, purple grey;
    and unto the rubber earth beneath.

And I knew then all I'd know for near half-an-hour:
    the blur of fast-passing light
    along the revolutionary's road,
    through Temple street,
    and the lane owed to a Ballaghaderreen man.

ERIC WEISKOTT

# Two Poems

## LANDFALL

In the dream you type and type until the other coast materializes. Out the porthole, fog and foghorn have reached a truce. What was once deleted can never be deleted again. Stroke, stroke, stroke. Gaze at the horizon if the nineteenth century makes you dizzy. Turn to crimson for the end of the day. Grab a pail and get to work on abstract expressionism. Are you always this insufferable? In dreams you don't have to answer that.

## EPITAPH

Here lies all your scholarship. Here lies your poetry.

In 1869, no monument was erected in honor of William Langland at St. Mary's parish church, Shipton-under-Wychwood, Oxfordshire.

No one strides across the Church Green in Shipton on one misty afternoon.

In 2022, after protracted debate, residents of Padua voted not to memorialize the setting of the *Taming of the Shrew* with a tourist center.

In the same year, the University of Padua celebrated its octocentenary.

Illyria, the untamed country, exists on the stage.

Here lies Geoffrey Chaucer. Because he was the first to be buried in Poets' Corner, one could not say Chaucer was buried in Poets' Corner. They buried him in a corner.

Your letter reaches me at a difficult time. I am celebrating my octocentenary as we speak.

A lineage of male surnames could be said. Here lies a lineage beneath the South Transept of Westminster Abbey. Chaucer, Spenser, Drayton, Dryden, South, Johnson, Campbell, Browning, Tennyson, Hardy, Kipling. Laurence Olivier.

You buried Charles Dickens with the poets. Here lies Mr. Dickens.

Here lies Gilbert Murray and Sullivan. Here lies the nineteenth century.

Here lies the horse you rode in on, Elizabeth Willis. Here lies the water you couldn't make him drink.

Here lies the fin de siècle.

Keats takes the form of an epitaph. Here lies the inscription of a surname in water. Is it the same water?

The unnamed country lies south of here. The epitaph is illyrical.

Here it lies. This epitaph is engraven upon Geoffrey Chaucer, father of poetry.

In 1929, no monument was erected to the future world war. Each year in our history is an interwar year. Each father in our lineage is a name.

Letters in the names had already melted off the face of the ice cliff before we arrived.

Here lies lifelikeness in fiction. Here lie Roland Barthes Simpson.

Here lies the unknown. Following this is our postwar period.

In 1869 at the intersection of First Street and South Street in Greenport, New York, not a damn thing happened. Here lies your maritime history. Here lies the North Fork of Long Island, tending northward into sound, formerly administered by the New Haven Colony. Here lies your souvenir shop. What follows is a chanty administered by the sons of colonial subjects.

Here lies your historical memory. Your problematic monument to Christopher Columbus. You can bring a statue to water, but you can't make it sink.

Here lies your statute. Residents voted. In 2024, after protracted debate: what follows.

K Weber

# Going Home

That foul toile upholstered
the bolsters and papered
too much news to the walls.
There was already enough

of our home's history. Who
knew a vintage pattern
could hunger and eat all
the young? Up-end vertigo

as a side-wound somersault?
My inner ears were dizzied
with truths that lived in this
stomach already. Ache emerged

from memory, its mouth; sharp,
bee-poked reminders of bleeding
gums and unspoken, argument-
carved words. I still hide behind

the heft of curtains, of eyelids.

Eric T. Racher

# Three Poems

## On the ideology of the sonnet
## considered as a form of 'communication'

Colloquial engeisted gloss beknown
erknown in contiguities that split
and fuse unparaphrasably to fit
unbraced-for circularities its own
and others' ablative *out of* there sown
in which the furies of erasure sit
has up *conatum* innerest of writ
and interstices optatively sewn.
But yet so for though if since thus i.e.
the *volta*'s overhearing overhear
we of ourselves influx of ear through which
such ontological porosity
as words bestow upon the spirit's sheer
negation might its own displacements pitch.

## On the ideology of language
## considered as a form of 'communication'

O heart us then and rhyme us in thy day,
as liveforevered as those words that circle,
self-organizing and self-replica-
ting, self-engendering in latticework
of patterns all sonnetted-up, though Burke
once warned of our propensity to weigh
all things against ourselves, our views, our works,
for the mirror holds us in its tempting sway.
If language fig-leafs us, a garment sewn
of labour, love and light (No mere discrete
communication system, neither just
a means of information transfer.), then
we do not language lettered utt'rance; it
is language languages unlettered us.

# Five love sonnets with rhymes stolen from Louis Zukofsky's "A"–9

### 1.

convention truth-likeness like's lie lies faded
memory repetition as a semblance
of itself as tautology's ear aided
by the eye perceives ordering resemblance
as rhythmic pulse representation values
lie lied lay the ear takes on labor is labor
*har ha-karmel* 2012 sunset all hues
over hills and the in-all-hues and the neighbor-
ing arc of sea's innate in us the light is
the sight as insight and memory mentors
us the beloved image is this night is
this light is magnanimity frequenters
toward toward the name name that exchanges
this lack for plenitude upturns arranges

### 2.

re-arranges landscape-turnings imaged changes
detailed in salutations and the real
the peal of laughter afterward estranges
nacreous demotic of the body ideal
askesis of the body askesis-token
*symbolon* baltic waves northlight induces
a blue even bluer still remains has been broken
by your touch as a colloquy produces
semblances of atemporal rose loci
loci mnemosyne holds light reflected
cathexis-dendrite mycelium sea rose-high
internal state the mysterion effected
*che ven da core* body and sea'd envision
there demarcated borne on such precision

### 3.

dream of transcendent hunger this prevision
vision measured in body wind sea or any-
one's-pine that was or olive no decision
olive I love or the no-one's-olive many
the *senhals* of your name but sea yours solely
and of it hidden mind's sudden sea senses
skin hand breast taste tongue chiselled into wholly
unbroken latitudes the dark's offenses
long last turned back at last heart self-extorted
nervous entanglements of self-impeded
soul's autoimmune disorders there exhorted
to myths of grace and gravity self ceded
to self self ceded yet to other decreases
what gyre turns us turn back to love's increases

## 4.

increase as sonnets' obsession psalms preces
back tossed and forth abundance carve curve into
skin of my palm shin of my psalm balm ceases
psalm psalmed psalming uniquenesses all thin to
spring desert waters infirmities torn a
skin vellum written upon take eye eyed eying
turn torn and tarnish fragilities' bourne a-
loft borne one shadow's one axiom's espying
these pained entelechies engraved behoove us
looming in twilight dawn of sea's appearing
daughters daughters of daughters sons loss prove us
psalmed loss love love a foreign body searing
love-strength lucid as dew *eshet-hayil* locus
o thou minist'ring angel turn-psalm focus

## 5.

tendernesses sea virtue value cloak us
living you love sea-marine acqua unguarded
sea-girded measured motion love invoke us
need evokes leewardings abstract discarded
lines love kisses hand deixis *cuore* asserted
one breath eyes sea is sea you you thus enjoined to
external cause the idea asserted averted
granite stands monumentalities point to
due season all alignments bear division
worded as chance occasion or a coded
conceit a being-next-to pure presence vision
love's closenesses transmuted uncorroded
horizonings of blazon's sense evaded
light's light you you thus equated equated

Abbie Hart

# Three Poems

## scamp

now that i
think about
it i do not th
ink i have ac
tually seen
a squirrel in
several weeks
i think i
would know b
ecause they do
n't really sc
amper they
just kind of
roll around as
if they were in
flated like ballo
ons and dart in
front of you wh
en you have fr
ies but i supp
ose like mysel
f they thought
the snow was
lovely at first
but have now
found that the
y haven't gott
en out of bed b
efore 4pm in 3
days.
(maybe it's seasonal.)

# BIRDHOUSE

i wish that my head looked like the inside of woodstock's birdhouse in merry christmas charlie brown.

from what i recall, it was midcentury modern and had a lovely little music box and maybe if i was alone inside my own head with no one to speak to no one would wish that i would stop talking.

there is a shag rug and it is pink and sometimes it whispers to me do you want to hear what it says good because i would have told you anyways because it tells me that one day i will leave and i will never see any of you again and i will be so happy so much happier than i have ever been.

i look into the mirror in the corner and it shows nothing because sometimes i forget what i look like and of course it's not a real mirror and it's letting me pretend that i am not who i always have been for a moment it is a lovely illusion.

you are not allowed in but when you inevitably show up can you please wipe your feet on the mat outside so that maybe my shag rug will begin to like you a little more.


# CHEESE BREAD WINE

i am making an offering to the god of make me forget i ever knew in hopes that i can leave and forget who i was enough to forget who i was enough for me to never come back again so i am leaving wine on the altar of let me pretend that i was not preyed on at age fourteen a slice of bread on the altar of let me forget that i saw another student being resuscitated a glass of wine on the altar of let me stop remembering that my ex had a tongue kink the flames lick at the feet of the little table of all of the things that will disappear into ash and they are gone and i let them go and maybe for once things start going in the right direction for me.

Juhan Oh

# Four 20ᵗʜ-Century Korean Poets: Yoon DongJoo, Yoo Chiwhan, Kim Sowol, and Kim Chunsu

## Foreword

### Yoon DongJoo (1941.11.2)

Looking up to the sky till the day I die
hopefully without a regret in mind–
even by a wind rustling the leaves
I suffered.
With a heart to sing the stars
I must love all dying things
and walk the path
given to me.


Once more the night stars are touched by the wind.



## Flag

### Yoo Chiwhan

This is a silent clamor
waving towards the big blue sea
everlasting nostalgia's handkerchief
pure love waves in the wind
at the end of the pole of clear ideology
grief spreads its wings as a white bird.
Oh, who is it.
That hangs such a sad and sorrowful feeling
up in the air.

# A Night Counting The Stars

## Yoon Dongjoo (1941.11.5)

In the sky passing the season
is filled with Autumn.

Without a doubt in mind
I might count all the stars inside Autumn.

The reason I can't count all the stars
written into my heart now
Is the reason morning comes so slowly,
the reason why night is still left,
the reason why my youth hasn't gone yet.

With a star, a memory
with a star, a love
with a star, an emptiness
with a star, a bow
with a star, a poem
and with a star, mother, mother,

Mother, with each star I recite beautiful words one by one. The names of the friends I shared my desk with in school, names of young foreign ladies like Pae, Kyung, and Ok, the names of girls that have already become mothers, names of my unfortunate neighbors, pigeons, dogs, rabbits, mules, deer, Francis Jammes, Rainer Maria Rilke—I call upon names of such poets.

Such are too far away.
Like how stars are vaguely too far,
mother,
and, you are far away in the North.

I am puzzled and full of longing-
on top of these many hills filled with the stars
I wrote my name
and covered it with dirt.

It might be that the insects singing through the night
are the reason I'm sad for shy names.

But as winter passes and spring comes to my stars
just as how blue grass appears upon graves
atop the hill with my buried name
grass will grow like a boast.

# Self-Portrait

## Yoon Dong Joo (1939.9)


I turn around the mountain side to visit the lonely well of the meadow and stare at it alone.

Inside the well, the moon shines, clouds flow, the sky unfolds, blue winds pass by and there is Fall.

And there is a stranger.
I feel a deep hatred for the stranger and go back.

Going back, I find myself pitying the stranger.
At the well, the stranger is still there.

Again, somehow I despise the stranger and go back.
Going back, I find myself longing for the stranger.

Inside the well, the moon shines, clouds flow, the sky unfolds, blue winds pass by, Fall is there, and the stranger is there like a warm memory.


# Azalea Flower

## Kim Sowol

When you get disgusted by looking at me
and go
I'll let you leave quietly without a word.

The mountain at Yung-Byun
azalea flowers
I'll pick a batch and spread them in your path.

With each step
stomp on the flowers
gracefully as you go

When you get disgusted by looking at me
and go

I'll not shed a tear, even if I die.

# A Flower

## Kim Chunsu

Before I called his name
he was nothing but
a faint gesture.

When I called his name
he came to me
and became a flower.

As I called his name,
someone, fit for my light and fragrance,
someone—call out my name.
I wish to go to him
and become a flower.

All of us
want to be something.
You to me, me to you
want to become one unforgettable glance.


# Confessions

## Yoon Dongjoo (1942)

In the copper mirror with blue rust
my face still being there
what kind of kingdom's relic is it
to be this cruel.

To shorten my confessions into one line:
24 years and 1 month,
what joy have I lived for.

Tomorrow or the day after, on any joyful day,
I must write another line of my confessions.
Why at such a young age
have I made such an embarrassing proposition.

Every night I clean my mirror
with my bare hands and feet.

Then a sight of a lonely man
walking below a meteorite
appears inside the mirror.

# An Easily Written Poem

## Yoon Dongjoo (1942.6.3)

The rain outside the window whispers
and this small room is a stranger's land,

despite knowing that a poet is a sad destiny
shall I write a line for my poem,

receiving the envelope with my college expenses
smelling pleasantly of sweat and love,

I grab my college notes
and go to listen to an old professor's lecture.

Thinking about it, when I was young
I lost all my friends one by one–

what do I wish for,
I am but—why am I plummeting down alone?

They say life is supposed to be difficult
but poems being this easy to write
is truly a shameful thing.

The rain outside the window whispers
and this small room is a stranger's land,

grab my lamp to push away the darkness,
the one waiting for morning to come, as if waiting on a century is the final me,

I reach out my small hand to myself,
with tears and relief, I reach for my first handshake.
*June 3rd, 1942*

# Schlagobersiana

## Schlagobers, But Only Sometimes

Eruptions can be dangerous, sometimes.
Stinky air is often, sometimes and always dangerous.
These insects! These birds!
They don't even know their own names! Ever!

Ping!
Stinky air is often, sometimes and always exquisite.
Flautists' wrenches invariably differ from that of
pipefitters' wrenches (spanners).
Ping!
Horologists' wrenches invariably differ from that of
pipefitters' wrenches (spanners).
Ping!

Each player gets a bean and a turn (and on April Fool, a turd).
Each player puts his or her bean in an oven.
The beans don't even know their own names, ever,
nor should they. The oven dwells in ignorance, always.
Players who forget their own names
often and sometimes consult their drivers' licenses
or other billfold information for that as well as
home addresses and phone numbers,
as well as, often and sometimes, home addresses, always.

## Your Parquet Floors

If you take a poet into your home,
be aware: he may not be housebroken.
We recommend spreading newspaper on your
parquet floors. When he has an "accident,"
grab him by the back of the neck
and rub his nose in the mess.
If he persists, return him to the breeder.

## Heresy

If I squirt a deity at a lesser deity
where will I spend eternity?

## Perched

His chief, smiling, the boy fell dead.
Perched. By God's grace. Nay, sire, killed.
All but shot in 2, off windowsills,
off kilter, catty-corner

with hard-boiled eggs
and a cloudless sky

## Sniffs

In the evening, over drinks? A McMansion
flirtation? A quickie on your ottoman?
Or better yet, a rock you pick up
thinking it's me?

## Magic Lantern

An off-label phenomenon offers its tongue
for inspection. Trying to guess why
is like knitting snot.
A magic lantern would help.

## My Rockets

My rockets, midflight, pause to preen.
My grenades whisper a wish:
to fondle avocados.

## Tiptoe Away

When you hear the dark angel snarling
unhand whatever impulse obtains
and tiptoe away.

## Autobiographical Tercet

Prudence's command,
"Unhand Imprudence!"
wobbles my creep.

César Dávila Andrade

# Five Poems

translated by Jonathan Simkins

## Limitless Trove

Between two sojourns
in the plaster asylums of the Moon,
I chanced upon that fetching rubble
of precious stone
enflamed by Hermits
in the center of their hearts
during Meditation.

Shard of the Mirrors of the Most High,
you disseminate Nothing
like the thirst of a hole
between the lips of the soul;
and Life,
like the tip of a needle
nailed to the stump of a Twinkle!

## Ouroboros

Only the instant betrays flawless time
before the swallows of the water clock abolish it.
Multitudes of mouths cry their lofty words:
"Mother, Death, Coño!"
Those souls evolve invariably identical to themselves,
in spite of their reverberating drunkenness.

I know of one who loves you with her pair of breasts, Ouroboros.
The curvy choirs of Night behold themselves in You,
mouth with tail.

Enveloped by the everlasting now of Love and Snow,
you repose, appraised by the incessant wheel.
Male and female in a spherical bed,
you bite, in turn, the gateway of the heart.

Fixed day, perpetually exterior to Time,
where does your Angel of prey gyre?
We've wandered far and wide for your dark atom,
but our soul has flashed its lightning.
Your puny Mondays, your tawdry and waxen Tuesdays,
we've attired them in seasons and anniversaries,
but they've received the gift of the Angels with frigid hands.
For a single pore of Eternity we have gazed on your Sundays,
and space still lingered for a splintered day.

O Time,
rekindle our memory of shedding our robes
at the feet of that lamp called Love,
when our bedbugs scurried helter-skelter
like our sisters under their umbrellas,
girls of summer reposing beyond sleep,
and all that remained was our spirit in the Grand Beyond.

Only you sleep, Motion, to envisage Time.
There in the eternal day nothing transpires.

Every eve dishevels our souls.
And everything around us reveals something within us.
The sparkling rubbish of sacred rings
recovers, furtively, our precious refuse,
our corpuscles of mysterious love.

O solitary Time,
in your successive void, we reclaim our faces
to smile on a world that isn't ours.

## At the Crest of the Bamboo Compass

Sole and swollen dawns
      the Herb of Daybreak,
powerless to swallow the moon,
its throat
a far cry from the mystical rubber of pregnancy,
but like a half-chilled bell
it preserves the lustre of the lion's den.
      Its metal
shimmers on the shiny old knee
      of Satan.
Rose of leather weathered by the atriums,
Rose of the beggars
and of prostitutes that bloom from columns.
      Skull on skull,
the world of the dead
swells the plastered honeycomb of Jehosaphat,
and his angels are sculpted by a waterfall.
Nevertheless,
with a flash of sight
the universe can be paused
and revised
like a clock that lifts its wings before chirping.

# ORIGIN

Now I know I was endowed with this soul in the heat of battle.
I saw my mother's cadaver under the Swan who loved her,
conjured by malefic matches.

I came to differentiate myself from you, Kinfolk,
Minerals, Archangels.
My infancy was never yours.
I fed alone, like a stray mirror
at the back of a forest.

My crib was the banquet in the ball of clay.
I devoured the knees of my wet nurse.
I slurped the voluminous eyes of women
who saw me emerging from an angel,
and received me in the raiment of the white caterpillar.

Amidst far-flung hosts and hereditary names
I fought,
bloodied by Mercy and Crime.
(O dreadful eve of arriving in the World with the executed.
Submerged in matter, the fervor of the Most High ceases.)

My mother entered every distance of the room.
Before my birth and after my departure,
a man was aging in the level litter of the saints.
He gazed on his coffin of cornwood,
preening himself with a giggling comb of bone,
gravely swilling his coffee
as if he were dying with every sip.

What terror fell from the rain-soaked flanks of the school.
The mass was freighted like a ship with wood and fire,
and the bell suffused every corner of the room
like a dew, under threat and on the lam.

Those holidays will never come again!
I stashed my cowhide rucksack in the barn.
I donned a blue sombrero in the backdrop of a photo
on a mountainous day of December
in the paper glade of an evening.
Farewell.

Those holidays we frolicked in the meadows!
Beforehand,
the puppy tinkled on a hidden flower,
steadying one leg in a precarious patch of paradise.
Puny ears of grain nibbled my mother's skirt
and escorted her to bed.

While the night endures

74

the most alluring rubble courses through the field.
Trees stoop down unseen
to cull the bliss of moistened arrows.
Hoary bulls chew the cud inside their sphinxes;
ancient muleteers converse with sleepless horses
before the ruin of the dawn's first rays.

Innocence, the immense eyes of domestic animals
beheld you with the sadness
of deceived pawns
uncoupled from intercourse.

My parents:
I know that in your ceremonial vessel
you fashion, hidden from the children,
wretched dalliances of the flesh
which debase you every morning.

Your hands, my parents,
reek of pelts expelled by the Sea:
Farewell.

On the dark rumps of the Indian maids
your lashes will be graven
like the zebra's skin wobbled by a bolt of Lightning.
Farewell.

Tend well, then, the forage crops, the ejidos,
the tombs;
the streetlights that dangle their acid globes
over the rows of hovels
in the Nights of San Juan.
Farewell.

Behold:
our father's seventh wife is stripping off her clothes,
the hair on her belly like the ace of black hearts in her bed.

There are acts of divination in the slenderest of portals.
Listen:
The adults are coming to die amid the white torrent of their sheets.
They are coming to chain us until dawn.

We set forth:
We are birthed in a sequential sky,
in plumage heaped on the Queens by the Ancient Sower.
But the light from the creases of his hand
wakes us penniless, like a gorgeous face
we knew a thousand years ago.

I too dreamed.
I saw a woman winding webs of purple cloth
around the pallid scepter of her soul.

I spoke with the idolatrous damsels who polish their throats
before they are drowned in the ponds of the Theologians.
Sullen clowns scraped the powder from their skin
to show me their imploring ulcers.
I watched dwarves stumbling
under the wings of the skaters.
I heard the howling of the tea the shipwrecked Captains
swilled amid the sobs of their final evening.
I gazed on columns stammering before the sun.

A hundred ages past,
I partook of a mystic love which I've forgotten,
and I am he no longer. Waves of time ago inside of Time,
I was summoned to the frontier of the Elders,
where I was furnished with my shadow.
I am no more the one you hid inside the Ovary
of the Illustrious Seated Statue
on rainy afternoons of the Ecuadorian South!
Nor am I still the one you stashed beneath a cloud of false witnesses
before the passage of the naked and disheveled woman
who flitters over adolescent eyelids.

Nonetheless, someone must remain shackled to the tresses
that blossom from the spring of the Savage Mother.
Someone must continue writing with their finger in the sand.
Someone must maintain the hunt
for parrots through a leafless sky.
Someone must preserve the hymn of the Chiaroscuro Man of the Night.
Someone must sustain the death throes of the Elders
on the itinerant table and its linen of corn.

## In an Unidentified Place

Do I seek the World of wood pulp,
or of the One
which has been whirling ten thousand years
on the knee of The Thinker?

Mothers of Milk,
the child who sobs for you
you suckled at the bosom.
You chose the deepest chamber of the house
for that, and to give birth
at the base of a waterfall,
like the does of the mountains!

The terror of the infinite enfolding you,
I love you my ultraviolet Beast.
With feathery hells I forge the lustre of the Ocean,
and I love you—once more—my Beast.

Amid the novel gas of violins, one could hear

—one could discern Oneself—.
It's the seamless grievance of the insect
munching a leaf perched on the race's urine.

Shelling corn in the night, they chant
for him
the shard of his soul dwelling in the foliage.
There isn't yet a grain of dust in the cavity of his thorax,
or a scratch of sun on his meninges;
but there
already beats the fish to come,
the bygone minotaur,
the whirling worm of the compass.
Unipedal animal in the yellow dust of the Bible.
Cryptogamic host, you blossom and increase,
as is feared of you: to be a true son!

Auriferous sands in the darkness of the Reading Room.
A grain of salt at the center
of the motherland's circumference,
the affliction of the Ecuadorian South.
Your Indian laundress
wrung out wells of water on the stone gods.

And in a sudden flash, millennia
of temporal Space have ceased.
Now coming and departing
will avail for you,
in the crimson mien of asbestos.
Who after one of us
will endure as the same
or the other forevermore,
to sustain the unalloyed elements
of Nothing?

The One who has been lost among the many,
and who opposes all of them
without his presence being known,
arises from a Place destroyed within Himself,
by virtue of a swift return
without escaping from the Current.
He has arisen from the sanguine fact
to trample his flesh in the pool of midday shade.
O Nadir of the pallid marshes!

And at once, He—the Singular—
gets cracking at grilling weeds like a man bewitched,
and foists on his parents
the death they had devised for Him
during their amorous liaisons with enormous reptiles,
a burial
in the sweetest slime of dawn!

Frost,
you glister on the umbrellas of the acrobats:
even my solitude
in the platinum mountains of Aldebaran
was slighter still than you.
While the Shyster Lords lunch with their ladies,
at the back of the City I nail
the sheepskin in which I was born.
And I am freed!

The aroma of a harlot's bed harbors
the Universal Gravitation!

Through nightmares and fever, one could escape
by swimming through a wave in the sheets,
or by way of the walnut eyes
which staved off the transformation into wood
by dint of weeping.
But
could He be saved from the Mothers of Fear,
from moans ascribed to cereal boxes
buried at the world's inception?
Or from the heart to come that resonates in every corner of creation?
And did salvation come, perhaps,
from the manic propagation of the world, murmuring
Round Bacteria with the others?

In one corner sat the table of idols,
the receptacles of prayers
that flapped their ambivalent tongues
like a graft.
They were oblivious of their lot as puny cannibals
subject to the vicious bread of the planet. They were defiled
in the darkness,
clattering their tiny sacks
of milk and spices!

Before, when the manna was still falling,
it was gathered by the scalpers, and every flavor
was assigned to a distinct disease.
But
you,
you evoked the Tartars with your breakfast,
hating each other in the name of effigies and hemispheres.
Already in the days of the Inca Empire
you performed black sorceries
in the clay pot!

With your mouths glazed in cocoa
you set out to gaze on the slaughters of eclipses,
and
returning at midnight,
you spread banners steeped in the musts of beasts

on the lips of your little ones.
What burning hands then
before the snare of raucous hair
on the clay handle of the door of love!

With the skeleton outside as a mortar,
you raised the fortress—lofty city—
beside the mouths of the Ossuary,
leaving a space at the center
for the Public Abyss opened
by the Battle of Pichincha.

And when you arrived, a multitude greeting the Ocean,
you heard the crests of evolution and of exodus,
limestone of the solar world in its nimble clock
sustained by trillions of oviducts!

It was the Motherland pecked
by the zodiacal needles of the pelican;
the estate, the ether, the end!
They gave you safety, girths of misgivings,
suspicions and resentments, stone criteria
to enclose the son of the mollusk.

Yes,
once more they circumscribed you
against the sea, against the pure Ocean of Oceania,
against the water that pervades
blue fire with neither usury nor desire.
And I say:
—"Who were you, before Now,
at the base of the great skull
of the Universe, brimming with poppy seeds?
Before the seven forms of Being surfaced
on the punctured brow of Zoroaster?
—Who were you,
before the union of sperm and Love
in the gallbladder of the infrared Beast?"

You were oblivious to the sperm discharged by the Nebula
in the caverns of milk. You missed
the Spirit nibbling its first morsel
of flesh and corpuscles!
Ever since,
we orchestrate
        saliva
            murex
                stearin

Richard Kostelanetz

# Switches

Lighthouse.  House light.

Overturn.  Turnover.

Home run.  Run home.

Horses race.  Race horses.

Overtake.  Takeover.

Gunshot.  Shotgun.

Elsewhere.  Where else.

Inside people.  People inside.

Eating fish.  Fish eating.

Cannibals cooking.  Cooking cannibals.

Bulls eye.  Eye Bulls.

Working stiff.  Stiff working.

Alien feeling.  Feeling alien.

Bed cover.  Cover bed.

Switch off.  Off switch.

Fast dinner.  Dinner fast.

Outside.  Side out.

Mate first.  First mate.

First second.  Second first.

Overcome  Come over.

Wind up.  Up wind.

House boat.  Boat house.

Watch dog.  Dog watch.

Fish bait.  Bait fish

Enhanced appearance.  Appearance enhanced.

Fool you.  You fool.

Box out.  Out box.

Downfall.  Fall down.

Marriage ban.  Ban marriage.

Nail polish.  Polish nail.

Slice potato.  Potato slice.

Measure tape.  Tape measure.

Hyenas torture.  Torture hyenas.

Class clown.  Clown class.

Barf bag.  Bag barf.

License pleasure.  Pleasure license.

Sex object.  Object sex.

Resting stop.  Stop resting.

Basketball.  Ball basket.

Bleach blonde.  Blonde bleach.

Withholding esteem.  Esteem withholding

Bowling alley.  Alley bowling.

Strike dead.  Dead strike

Whore house.  House whose.

Broken string.  String broken.

Nursery rhyming.  Rhyming nursery.

Island treasure.  Treasure island.

Gesture strong.  Strong gesture.

Hits batter.  Batter hits.

Following her.  Her following.

Like war.  War like.

Loving good.  Good loving.

Outlook.  Look out.

Strike three.  Three strike.

Tired dog.  Dog tired.

Foot club.  Club foot.

Overrun.  Run over.

Concert music.  Music concert.

High jump.  Jump high.

Lunch hour.  Hour lunch.

Stupid acts.  Acts stupid.

Overcome.  Come over.

Ships sink.  Sink ships.

Motherfucking.  Fucking mother.

Doubt everyone.  Everyone doubt.

Jump high.  High jump.

Point blank.  Blank point.

Up higher.  Higher up.

Parade women.  Women parade.

Catholic converts. Converts Catholic.

Higher count.  Count higher.

Privilege genius.  Genius privilege.

Box safely.  Safely box.

Crying shame.  Shame crying.

Living rich.  Rich living.

Establish friendships.  Friendships establish.

Sounds mix.  Mix sounds.

Vegetarian eats.  Eats vegetarian.

Girls call.  Call girls.

Fake people.  People fake.

Acting dumb.  Dumb acting.

Fear thieves.  Thieves fear.

Film sex.  Sex film.

Fakes brilliance.  Brilliance fakes.

Seeing pretty.  Pretty seeing.

Rest assured.  Assured rest.

Wrong way.  Way wrong.

Better acting.  Acting better.

Wishing well. Well wishing.

Everyone believing.  Believing everyone.

Far reaching. Reaching far.

Too beautiful.  Beautiful too.

Point out.  Out point.

House shit.  Shit house.

Open doors.  Doors open.

Lying under.  Underlying.

Mice eat.  Eat mice.

Highest prize.  Prize highest.

Green painting.  Painting green

Savings bank.  Bank savings.

Money man.  Man money.

Link friends.  Friends link.

Writing machine.  Machine writing.

Empty trash. Trash empty.

Daily mail.  Mail daily.

Party school.  School party.

Love summertime.  Summertime love.

Fish hook.  Hook fish.

Friends disappoint.  Disappoint friends.

Recognizes intelligence.  Intelligence recognizes.

Combat ants.  Ants combat.

Queries puzzle.  Puzzle queries.

Me remembering.  Remembering me.

Food fight.  Fight food.

Feel good.  Good feel.

Ring finger.  Finger ring.

Deception projects.  Projects deception.

Hang man.  Man hang.

Extra charge.  Charge extra.

Close colleagues.  Colleagues close.

Rule out.  Out rule.

Weaker sister.  Sister weaker.

Electric light.  Light electric.

Cheating casinos.  Casinos cheating.

Aspiration wishes. Wishes aspiration.

Flat broke. Broke flat.

Wisely reading. Reading wisely.

Resigned look. Look resigned.

Working girls. Girls working.

Long ball. Ball long.

Dog tired. Tired dog.

Slice bread. Bread slice.

Coffee house. House coffee.

Wire live. Live wire.

Music concert. Concert music.

Crazy boy. Boy crazy.

Horseback. Back horse.

Train ride. Ride train.

Eyesore. Sore eye.

Long gone. Gone long.

Crowds announcing. Announcing crowds.

Certifying true. True certifying.

Going out. Outgoing.

Potato chips. Chips potato.

Execution summary. Summary execution.

Pitcher hits. Hits pitcher.

Ice hockey. Hockey ice.

Secure deposit. Deposit secure.

Optional choice. Choice optional.

Inside job. Job inside.

Garden sculpture. Sculpture garden.

Explained nothing. Nothing explained.

Barf bag. Bag barf.

Lion tamer. Tamer lion.

Food fair. Fair food.

Befriend strangers. Strangers befriend.

Breakfast.  Fast break.

Picture perfect.  Perfect picture.

Waking hours.  Hours waking.

Outside.  Side out.

Astrology predicts.  Predicts astrology.

Rare steak.  Steak rare.

Stupid move.  Move, stupid.

Closet gay.  Gay closet.

Banking community.  Community banking.

Car crash.  Crash car.

Examining doctor.  Doctor examining.

Wireless.  Less wire.

Program radio.  Radio program.

Male female.  Female male.

Smarts showing.  Showing smarts.

Seersucker.  Sucker seer.

People cross.  Cross people.

Cat house.  House cat.

Read books.  Books read.

Forward march.  March forward.

Forget people.  People forget.

Copywrite.  Write copy.

Pets torture.  Torture pets.

Smell skunks.  Skunks smell.

Endanger soldiers.  Soldiers endanger.

Heart bleeding.  Bleeding heart.

Highrise.  Rise high.

Storefront.  Front store.

Sheepskin.  Skin sheep.

Side street.  Street side.

Wolf cry.  Cry wolf.

## REVIEWS IN BRIEF | Charles Holdefer

### The Penult
### Colin Gee
### Leftover Books, 2023

In these stories, many of which are set in Mexico, where the author resides, Gee shows a fine ear for shifting tones, effects of register, and variety of *Englishes*. The principal landscape, though, is a liminal space of a surreal and comic imagination. Gee rewrites fairy tales and poems by Emily Dickinson; "Her Philosophy" is a mash-up of King James English and a posse of Missouri cowboys. These are sophisticated performances that manage to avoid being ponderously "literary" due to their wit. Arguably, these stories might be better served in the form of several books, or chapbooks, reflecting Gee's multifarious voices. On the other hand, *The Penult* has the virtue of gathering a highly original author's work in one place, and allowing the reader to see the breadth of his vision.

### Even So
### David D. Coster
### Ice Cube Press, 2024

This coming-of-age memoir centered on the author's youth growing up in a family of ten. Nostalgic reminiscences of life on the farm soon cede place to considerable darkness, as death and abuse enter the picture. Coster's father, a talented, cruel, driven man who literally tilts at windmills, and his mother, isolated by otherworldly Pentecostal beliefs as she negotiates multiple childbirths, are described with frankness and a remarkable lack of bitterness. As a young gay man fighting to acquire an education (he later became a surgeon), David Coster has a fascinating story to tell. The latter chapters, in particular, are full of riveting moments, and *Even So* is an impressive debut.

## REVIEWS IN BRIEF | Jesi Bender

### Cardboard Clouds
### Benjamin Niespodziany
### X-R-A-Y Lit, 2023

This collection of short (page-length) plays is surreal and complex despite its minimalist leanings. Firstly, it's important to note that this is one of the most beautiful books, as an object. Perhaps the best aspect of its content is how it plays two forms against each other: theater and literature. The plays often set up contradictory actions and impossible staging, creating the otherworldly atmosphere of these 'nowhere/at no time' performances. Each page/play with its existential questions and paradoxical scenarios reinforces the performance of identity, specifically its creation and its destruction.

### Lord of Chaos
### Daniel Beauregard
### Erratum Press, 2023

*Lord of Chaos* is a novel that poetically embodies chaos and asks *who is its master?* Throughout the text, the story is told from the point of view of "we"—which is technically first-person but also is a way to meld the narrator into both you and me. The origins of we, the bringing together of multiple perspectives, the plurality inherent in the universal, is where chaos originates. Philosophical and psychedelic, this text looks into the void and records everything that echoes back to us.

### Fish Cough
### Craig Buchner
### Buckman Publishing, 2023

In Buchner's debut novel, a couple named Thom and Howard have their stagnant relationship upended by a once-in-a-lifetime meteoric storm. Like the best magic surrealist novels Buchner deftly shapes the surreality of everyday life. Their lives are complemented by the magical events set in motion by the storm because life is already so bizarre. Everything that *couldn't happen* in real life seems at once both plausible a well as supernatural. More literary than genre this work exposes the horror in a regular life filled with aging and all its quotidian anxiety.

### Centrifugal: Unstories
### Matt Burnside
### Whiskey Tit, 2024

I consider myself one of the world's foremos Matthew Burnside scholars and I want everyon to read him because he's brilliant. The king bittersweet, his latest collection is another lo letter to the lonely that uses familiar Burnsid paradigms of games, childhood, nautili, and digital universes. He experiments with the form in new and exciting ways that mirror modern or near-future life but also has enough 'traditional' structure to appeal to a wide audience. If you love stories that break your heart but also somehow lift you up out of that melancholy, you need more Burnside in your life.

## REVIEW | JOHN PATRICK HIGGINS

*Sun Eye Moon Eye*
Vincent Czyz
Spuyten Duyvil, March 2023

In the afterword of this book, and with admirable coolness, Vincent Czyz recounts the novel's thirty-two-year Odyssey, from pen to published. He tells of the hundreds of pages gutted from the text, the decades of encouraging rejections, the frustrated disappearance of agents. When his publication deal finally arrives, it sits unseen in his spam folder for a fortnight before being found by accident. In the face of this, one can only speculate on what Vincent Czyz did to anger the gods, what it was he thrust hubristically into their faces, and how he had the resilience to continue. Odysseus, remember, was safely returned home and casually murdering his wife's suitors in a third of the time.

A flower that blooms every three decades is a rare one indeed, and this is an *Agave Americana* of a novel: big, insistent, fibrous and with prickly marginalia.

The novel places us in the elemental world of Logan Blackfeather, a musician of mixed Hopi descent, dealing with the suspected murder of his father by his troll-like uncle, Cal. Cal is described as from the moon and made of it. Dull, grey, inert, he is a crushing, silent weight on the couch, his face blue and unblinking under cathode rays, as beer cans sweat between his enormous fingers. Worse, he has taken Logan's father's place in the family home, which he rules with a fist of granite. Logan dreams of killing him.

Years later, after a mescal epiphany in the desert, and the efficient killing of a racist trucker, Logan finds himself in a hospital with a

"Don't let anyone tell you otherwise: The world exists to break to your heart.

Some deal with this fact by breaking it back. Others just end up breaking themselves.

A few, who are somehow able to accept what's broken, may find a way to be grateful to it.

These people are called fools."

cast of comic psychiatric patients, under the care of an 80's smooth physician, Aristotle Manolokas. Logan escapes, heads to Manhattan, cutting his long hair as a symbolic break with the past. Here he meets punks and yuppies—both openly mocked—and several women who find him incredibly attractive. He favours Shawna, a successful advertising executive, and drifts into her glitzy, bohemian milieu, sneering at the people he meets there.

This is a novel of parts. Logan searches for his identity in the desert, feeling distant from and alienated by his native heritage. He is desperate for rapture, to surrender to the earth, to be accepted by his ancestors, but he's sloughed off, discarded, found unworthy. Conversely, this country boy walks city streets with total confidence. Nothing fazes him. The city is not worthy of him. He sees its vapidity, its empty constructs, its lack of truth. The people are pitiful too. The punks aping native costume are laughable, the soft-handed, coke-addled money-brokers, objects of scorn. Yet it's here, in these cement canyons, his father's ghost appears: companionable, shorter than Logan remembers, a good guy. It's one of the stranger moments in the book. In this story, the sun eye shows detail, exactitude, colour and logic, all the Apollonian virtues. The moon eye reveals murky, liminal places, a hypnogogic Etch A Sketch, readily re-written. There's rarely balance, but it's there when Logan meets his father's ghost for the second time. The first time he was unknowable, mute, a freakish projection, utterly moon-eyed. This time he's a buddy. They share a beer. There's even some slight closure. For a book that blazes with visionary fire—Logan's world can be brutal, as can he— it's a quiet moment, a cool afternoon.

Czyz excels at the gritty verity of eighties New York, and the rapturous language of euphoria and both these things melt into the transcendent final chapters of the book, as Logan—falling upwards—becomes an accidental rock star, ferried around a high-end New York art party as though by Virgil, through concentric circles, gaudy and tight as a coiled serpent, an ouroboros lustily consuming itself with the powdery vigour of Patrick Bateman in a mirrored toilet cubicle. The scene becomes hazy, nebulous, the writing heightened and dazzling. It's an astonishing denouement, the narrative melting away, until we're left in another kind of desert, populated by phantoms, by tricksters, by the dead, where language is mere symbols smeared on a crumbling wall, and the fallen arches of Ozymandias are consumed by sands, and Logan is finally home.

This book was worth the wait. In gold.

REVIEW | Kurt Luchs

# Two Firesigns, Three Books

*The Sullen Art: Recording the Revolution in American Poetry*
David Ossman
University of Toledo Press, 2016

*The Old Man's Poems: 75 Views of Mt. Baker*
David Ossman
Egress Studio Press, 2019

*Tales of the Old Detective and Other Big Fat Lies*
Philip Austin
Bear Manor Media, 2021

The Firesign Theatre was a four-man American comedy troupe that came together in November 1966 and stayed active, with many side journeys and interruptions, until 2012 when founding member Peter Bergman died. Phil Austin then passed in 2015. David Ossman and Phil Proctor are the only two surviving members. While the group worked extensively in radio and on stage, and to a lesser degree in film, they are chiefly remembered for inventing a new kind of comedy album, one that took complete advantage of the modern recording studio to create works of remarkable depth and complexity. This is why they have been called "the Beatles of comedy."

The Firesign Theatre was important, even central, to the youth culture and counterculture of the sixties and seventies. To give just one example, they organized the first Love-In. They were also important to me personally, inspiring me to become a writer and to form my own comedy troupe with some of my siblings, the Luchs Brothers. I became friends with all of them to one degree or another, but in particular with Ossman. He was both a mentor and an exemplar to me of how a writer could keep one foot in the world of humor and the other in the world of poetry, something he has done with grace his entire career.

Although Firesign Theatre no longer exists as a group, Ossman has kept their work alive by getting virtually everything they wrote into print with Bear Manor Media. At the same time, he has continued to pursue one of his other main interests, poetry. In the early sixties he worked in public radio at WBAI in New York, where he hosted "The Sullen Art," a groundbreaking series of interviews with American poets. The title of the program and the book drawn from it namechecked the Dylan Thomas poem "In My Craft or Sullen Art." In his introduction to the original 1963 edition, Ossman noted that the title "has no pejorative connotations . . . 'sullen' comes from the Latin solus—alone. These poets, and all poets, despite their contacts with the world, are ultimately alone. One creates, after all, by one's self."

The irony here is that three years after these words were published, Ossman began working with—and creating with—his three Firesign compadres. And all the while he maintained a career as a poet. He published a series of highly original chapbooks and several full-length collections. He also oversaw the reissue of *The Sullen Art* in an expanded edition from the University of Toledo

Press. The original 13 interviews have been doubled to 26. What was a meaningful sampling of the state of poetry in the early sixties, as it was in the midst of evolving, is now a comprehensive overview. Poetry has moved on, but this book has captured these poets in the act of making a literary revolution, or several revolutions, really. Its value as a historical document has only increased, and the CD included with the book gives a good taste of what these interviews sounded like on the radio.

One of the interviews added to the new edition is with Daisy Alden, founder of the influential fifties magazine *Folder*. She says this: "I'm very interested in the visual as well as the printed word. I think that having the poem or the story in an attractive setting is an important part of the literary experience." That is the ideal segue into a review of Ossman's latest book of verse, *The Old Man's Poems: 75 Views of Mt. Baker*. Like most of his poetry collections, whether chapbook or full-length, it's a work of art as well as literature, beautiful to behold and to read. Publisher Anita K. Boyle has adorned the text with six woodcuts that complement the poems perfectly. The book contains handmade paper and is handsewn. Although technically a paperback, the covers are of stiff cardboard overlain with a cardboard jacket, giving the effect of a hardcover. Anyone who loves the lost art of bookmaking will love this book.

More importantly, the book itself is more than worthy of the presentation. These poems are incomparably Ossman's best, a fine distillation of everything he has been and done and known and is. A prefatory note makes clear his debt to classical Chinese verse—specifically, the book *Five Tang Poets* assembled and translated by David Young. Ossman's idea was to write a series of nature lyrics using Mt. Baker as the focal point, celebrating his 75th birthday, which for the record was December 6, 2011. The poems were written between 2010 and 2012; the book did not appear until 2019. The mountain and the old man are the two main foils until a kitten shows up partway through.

Such a simple setup, about as simple as *Waiting for Godot*, yet Ossman finds so many ways to

"make it new," as Pound said. The language is direct, spare and supple, capable of many effects, such as sudden beauty:

> bright piece out of pale sky
> Mountain slips away      then
> the bone Moon      struck      the bay

There is also warmth, sentiment and humor:

> old man's boys give a gift
> of kitten
> infinitely smaller than
> Mountain but
> with the same sharp claws

As one might expect in a book inspired by Chinese poetry, there are occasional sparks of Buddhist thought:

> Mountain is there and not-there
> the habit of mountains

In this case I believe he's referring to D. T. Suzuki's *Essays in Zen Buddhism*, a book he certainly knows. Yet he could also be thinking of the charming calypso-infused Donovan song from 1967, "There Is a Mountain" ("First there is a mountain / then there is no mountain / then there is"). The outside world presses in at times—there are several references to the then-current war in Afghanistan—but the framing of everything in the shadow of the mountain, and the shadow of the cat, keeps these lovely poems grounded in a much more personal present. The book is divided into seasons, again something typical of classical Chinese verse. Then, too, within the seasons are times of joy and grief. He includes one poem about the son of his who died on a different mountain, Mt. Rainier. And there are moving elegies for his Firesign partner Peter Bergman and his creative mentor Ray Bradbury.

Ossman's poetic roots go in many directions. However, I think his work has felt the strongest influence from the Black Mountain poets, especially Robert Creeley, as well as Gary Snyder and Hispanic poets such as Federico Garcia Lorca, some of whose work Ossman took it upon himself to translate. Like Yeats, he just keeps topping himself.

*Tales of the Old Detective and Other Big Fat Lies* by Philip Austin began life as an audiobook in 1995. I wrote about it for the audiobook newsletter I was producing at the time, *Talking Book Review*. I was delighted when the publisher asked me and Chevy Chasc for cover blurbs and even more delighted when he gave mine top billing (after all, I'm Kurt Luchs and he's not). In 2021, six years after Austin's death, this almost-lost classic became a book proper, thanks to Bear Manor Media. There's a brief, poignant introduction by the author's widow, Oona, the "big beautiful blonde" sometimes mentioned in these deliciously noir and surreal stories.

"The Old Detective" referred to here is clearly a later version of Firesign Theatre's best-known character, Nick Danger, played and co-written by Austin. The character draws on many sources, including old time radio programs like *Yours Truly, Johnny Dollar*, and several hard-boiled mystery writers. More than anything, though, he comes as a response to the prose of Raymond Chandler. The group used to begin their writing sessions by reading his work out loud. Firesign's last studio album for Columbia Records was *In the Next World, You're on Your Own*, the only album performed by the group but written by the duo of Austin and Ossman. That album was dedicated to Jorge Luis Borges and Raymond Chandler, a dedication that would work equally well for this book.

These 17 stories can start anywhere and end anywhere, with plenty of strange doings in between. Take "We Three Kings of Tacoma Are," one of several surprisingly moving Christmas tales in the collection, which begins like this: "Not too many years past, in that region of the Pacific North where people have settled, wisely or not, around the base of the great volcano Tahoma, and specifically in the misspelled city of Tacoma, in the State of Washington—and on a dark and stormy night—the sodden figure of a drunken man fell to its knees in the humble neighborhood near St. Bart's mighty old dark brick church set high up one of the seven hills above the twisted mystery of the lower Puget Sound." Now *that's* an opening sentence! If you are any kind of red-blooded American you will want to know what happens next.

Or take "School Lunch Menus," a non-detecting bit that could have come straight from Fire-sign's *Dear Friends* radio series/album, and which opens like this:

PLAIN ELEMENTARY SCHOOL

MON: Paper stack; Boneless Burrito; Paste;Kitten on a stick; Milk-a-roni

TUES: White bread on toast; Glass of Sugar; See-through Lettuce; Liquid Milk

WED: Cake Sponge; Sugar Sandwich; Butter Plate; Cloth Pudding; Milk

THU: Simple Pie; Banana Splat; Sugar Mound; Blanched Cookie; Whey

FRI: Diaper Surprise; Clear Peaches; Steamed Cereal Boxes; Sugar; Milk

Someday, perhaps, Austin's long-awaited novel *Beaver Teeth* may become a book, and his screenplay about the Grateful Dead, two projects that have yet to see a real release. Until then, though, it's a genuine delight to have *Tales of the Old Detective and Other Big Fat Lies*, as pure a product of his unique imagination as we could wish for.

REVIEW | Kurt Luchs

*The Creative Act: A Way of Being*
Rick Rubin
Penguin Press, 2023

The situation for artists trying to learn how to be better artists is a microcosm of the human situation at this moment in time. The use of computers and cell phones along with the unending growth of the internet and streaming, and the globalization of the economy, have brought almost all extant human information to our fingertips. Yet having instantaneous access to nearly everything we've done as a species does not help us parse that bottomless pit of data into useful facts, knowledge, or—most necessary of all—wisdom. To put it another way, our culture (if that is the right word) is badly in need of curating. And many of us engage in that task by putting together literary magazines like *Exacting Clam* or writing reviews like this one. Some of us do craft talks as well, and heaven knows craft matters in art as in everything else.

All that is well and good. But what about the thing that precedes craft, the creative impulse itself? Can anything of real value be taught or studied or learned about that?

I am happy to report that the answer is yes. *The Creative Act: A Way of Being* reveals Rick Rubin to be the preeminent guru of creativity in our time. Not since *The Artist's Way* by Julia Cameron has anyone written a book so inspiring, accessible, useful and truly helpful to those of us laboring in the vineyards of the arts. Rubin is like a Zen master drunk on the beauty of art and sharing a thousand koans with his disciples out of a pure generosity of spirit.

Does it matter how he acquired this wisdom? Not really. But where he came from is interesting, if only because it might cause some people's heads to explode, trying to put his background together with the old soul that wrote this book. Rubin has been a producer of popular music for more than four decades. He was not only present at the birth of hip hop, he was one of the fathers as a co-founder of Def Jam recordings. He has worked with Run-DMC, the Beastie Boys, Public Enemy, Metallica, Aerosmith, Audioslave, the Strokes and Weezer, among countless others.

Most memorably, for my money, he found a niche working with popular artists who might appear to be all washed up creatively, coaxing out of them a renewed vision and some of their best work. I'm thinking here not only of Johnny Cash in his final incredible decade but also Donovan (*Sutras*) and Neil Diamond (*12 Songs*).

Many producers are known for a particular sound. For example, Laurie Latham, who worked with the Stranglers, Echo and the Bunnymen and Squeeze, can be spotted instantly by the hypnotic, layered gloss of the keyboards. Steve Lillywhite and Hugh Padham will forever be known as the producer and engineer (respectively) who created the "gated reverb" sound for Phil Collins' drums (with a little help from their friend Peter Gabriel).

While some have identified Rubin by what they call his stripped-down sound, I don't believe he has a personal sound at all. I think he has the much rarer gift of helping an artist look

within to find the best they are capable of. So yes, he is in some sense responsible for the Red Hot Chili Peppers. But then, as a uniquely selfless producer, he was simply helping them be the best Red Hot Chili Peppers they could be.

What a music producer has in common with other artists is the ability to listen, both inwardly and outwardly, to be fully attentive to the moment, with no preconceptions. For some insight into Rubin's ability to listen, check out his in-depth interview with Paul McCartney, available in three chapters on Hulu. At one point Rubin plays the recording of "While My Guitar Gently Weeps" from what has come to be known as the Beatles' White Album. It's a George Harrison song, of course, arguably the one that revealed his full maturity as a songwriter. The casual listener might think, "This is a groovy little number, nice guitar solo" (which in fact was played not by Harrison but by his pal Eric Clapton). Does the casual listener even hear the bassline played by Paul? Well, Rick Rubin does. As he and Paul listen to the original multitrack session tape with the bass track turned up, it's a revelation for the viewer. Paul's bass part is absolutely insane, like a whole different song going on within the song. And in typical Beatles fashion, it's the mix of these two elements, with the audacity of the bassline counterpoint just below the threshold of consciousness, that helps make the song so good.

Rubin goes on to note that no normal session musician would ever have played a bass part like that. His comment pertains both to Paul's virtuosity on his main instrument and also to the unusually open and nourishing creative environment within the Beatles, where Ringo or a roadie or a second assistant engineer could come up with a good idea and have it instantly accepted.

You might say that Rubin's goal with this book is to help every artist—indeed, every human being—attain this kind of openness within their own psyche. The epigraph he has chosen for the book is a good indicator of this: "The object isn't to make art, it's to be in that wonderful state which makes art inevitable" (Robert Henri). In other words, a way of being precedes the creative act.

The table of contents is not called that but rather "78 Areas of Thought." Right from the start, he declares that creativity is not something possessed only by artists, in a chapter called "Everyone Is a Creator." He states, "Creativity is a fundamental aspect of being human." Thus, while this book will get especially heavy use from painters, composers and writers, it will also provide tools for entrepreneurs to create new products and services, or coaches to create new plays for their teams. It really does have something for everybody. It is very tempting to simply go on quoting it endlessly but I'd much rather you make your own fruitful discoveries in its pages. Rick Rubin has earned his place on your bookshelf next to Julia Cameron. Make room for him.

## REVIEW | Adam McPhee

*Glorious Exploits*
Ferdia Lennon
Henry Holt and Co, 2024

Set after Athens' failed invasion of Sicily during the Peloponnesian War, *Glorious Exploits* by Ferdia Lennon is narrated by Lampas, an unemployed thirty-year-old Syracusan with a clubfoot. Laid off from the pottery factory, he spends his days accompanying his best friend Gelon to the local limestone quarry, now an open air prison camp where a few hundred defeated Athenian soldiers are slowly starving to death.

Gelon, haunted by the loss of his wife and child—she ran off after they lost the child to disease, proving there's still plenty of tragedy outside of the war—goes to the quarry in search of snippets of Athenian tragedy, which he's mad for, and the quarry, being full of Athenians, is a jackpot. Some of the soldiers have acting experience, and Gelon decides to use them to stage a production of Euripides' *Medea*, with Lampas joining him as co-director. Gelon and Lampas pay for the expenses—mostly they need food to keep the soldiers alive, but also set decorations and theatre masks—by selling the hoplite armour taken from some Athenian corpses discovered just off the side of the road.

Everyone suffers in this ancient world full of slavery, disease, violence, and lost loved ones. And the suffering is *vivid*: anyone can come up with a legless beggar singing for change, but there's something special, I think, about having the beggar actually sinking in the mud during a heavy rain.

Everyone suffers, but not everyone suffers equally. All social relations are explicitly hierarchical here, and the humiliation that comes from being reminded you're beneath a prosperous cousin with a stall in the marketplace or a snotty aristo kid slumming in your quarter goes a long way to explaining why characters sometimes react suddenly with what might otherwise seem like unprovoked casual violence: there's only so much humiliation a person can take. And yet life goes on, and there's tenderness, too: Gelon and Lampas are led to the hoplite corpses by a group of war orphans, and together they hold an impromptu and rather moving funeral for the Athenians, even though it's the Athenians who took the orphans' fathers.

The days of historical fiction filled with artificially stilted language, inevitably more Victorian than whatever era the author is trying to evoke, are coming to a close—and thank the gods for that. Still, the question of how people spoke to one another in the past is a central question that any such novel has to address. Do you create a 'shadow tongue' using Old English words and modern syntax, as Paul Kingsnorth did for *The Wake*? Or do you forgo that and use internet-inflected slang as Maria Dahvana Headley did for her *Beowulf*? Lennon opts for Irish-accented English, Hiberno-English I guess is the term and it works. These are, after all, working class characters speaking to each other in the local vernacular of an island that's been subject to a harsh attempt at colonization from a neighbour. Still, the intentional rhyming of 'cod' and 'god' is a little off-putting, a jarring misstep that reminds us the two languages don't actually overlap so neatly. Likewise, the continual mention of pockets brought to mind a Latin teacher I once had, an expert on the costumes of antiquity, who would rage whenever she came across a mention of pockets in historical fiction about Rome.

On the other hand, the novel's language regarding the theatre veers closer to Hollywood, and while the back of my mind was trying to check all this against whatever history I half re membered (did Ancient Greek Plays really have producers? Or casting sessions?), it ends up working in the context of the novel, and it's easy to just roll with it. Sure, there was probably some complex Greek technical term for a stagehand, but calling the orphans production assistants works fine, too.

At any rate, all historical fiction has to pull off a bit of a bait and switch, speculating about the past by subbing in a little of something from the present, and for what it's worth, *Glorious Exploits* does a better job at this sleight of hand than César Aira's *Fulgentius,* the other recent novel about amateur stage production in the ancient world. Here it's working class life that's subbed in, which manages to find a good mix between the familiar—performing banter in a tavern—and the alien: the novel's love plot involves Lampas falling for the slave girl who works as a barmaid in his favourite tavern, which of course raises a set of ethical questions that the novel then has to weave its way around without turning anyone into a 19th-century abolitionist or having the reader close the book in disgust. For the most part, it works.

The Athenian plays are only described in snippets, and when Gelon and Lampas decide to make the play a double bill they cut off the beginning of Euripides' recently released *Trojan Women,* because even the Athenian actors can't remember it, and yet their passion always shines through. Gelon and Lampas experience a real catharsis from these plays, and so, vicariously, do we. It explains why they're ready to move on from the war and get on with their lives: because catharsis is a purging of emotions. But Greek tragedy isn't distributed evenly, Lampas points out Syracuse is a bit of a backwater in that regard. And even though Syracuse has prospered—new buildings leave the city unrecognizable, and tour guides make coin showing foreigners the spot where Athenian general Nicias was beheaded—there's still a hateful, reactionary feeling popular with the locals, and they're not content with letting the Athenians starve to death. Ironically, the people who could most benefit from Athenian tragedy are those least likely to want to watch it—now that's tragedy.

This all erupts, of course, at the first performance of the play. And it would've been better to let the novel end there, or slightly thereafter. What comes afterwards is just melodrama, and while I have nothing against melodrama—I live for certain kinds of it—it's not going to hit as hard as a well-crafted piece of real tragedy, real drama. The Irish merchant-turned-producer feels a little too much like a mysterious recurring villain in a fantasy series (though I'm still thinking about his god in a fishtank), the prison break feels out of character for those involved (and I'm surprised the Athenians didn't try to pull something off themselves), and while the fate of Lyra the slave girl comes off as fitting and inevitable it's also somewhat lacking. It's revealed, Lampas reacts, and then the story just ends.

Still, the novel is worthwhile, and it's easy to see this becoming a staple for anyone looking to wrap their head around Greek theatre.

**REVIEW** | Eric Weiskott

# A Return to Form?

Ben Lerner
*The Lights*
Farrar, Straus, & Giroux, 2023

*The Lights* is Ben Lerner's return to verse form, after a trilogy of celebrated novels.[1]

I am grateful to Ben Paul for long discussions about Ben Lerner's poetry, which inform this essay.

Before the novels, Lerner published a trilogy of poetry books, culminating in *Mean Free Path* (2010). Since then, many readers, reviewers, and scholars have allowed themselves to think of Lerner as a novelist who once wrote poetry. This judgment corresponds to the market dominance of the novel form over poetry, the tendency of the former to displace the latter in contemporary literary culture, but in Lerner's case it always jarred against the prominence of lyric poetry in each of his novels. In the most well-known of them, *10:04,* the poet/novelist protagonist reads Walt Whitman and holds a residency in Marfa, Texas, where he composes Lerner's long poem about reading Whitman and holding a residency in Marfa, Texas, "The Dark Threw Patches Down upon Me Also." The poem undergirds the novel like the crossbeams of the Brooklyn Bridge, or rather the novel "dissolves into a poem," to borrow a phrase from *10:04* itself. First collected in *No Art*, which reprints the poetic trilogy alongside four newer poems, "The Dark Threw Patches Down upon Me Also" resurfaces in *The Lights*. Lerner's Whitman poem has traveled from poetry to novel back to poetry, and so has Lerner.

In a 2019 interview with Ocean Vuong, Lerner predicted that *The Topeka School*, published that year, would be his last novel. So far he has kept that promise. Readers of his poetry are now afforded the opportunity to think of him as a poet who once wrote novels. Yet that isn't quite right either, particularly since many of the poems in *The Lights* are medium-length prose dramas with scenes, characters, and dialogue, some so long that they first appeared in the *New Yorker* labeled "Fiction." Lerner's poetry has learned something from Lerner's fiction. The great longitudinal fissure between the poetry hemisphere and the fiction hemisphere is not so great in his case. Still, *The Lights* comes at a pivotal career moment for Lerner. It breaks the tie between poetry books and novels, and breaks it in poetry's favor. It remains to readers to take up the formal challenge implicit in the arc of Lerner's publishing career from the 2000s to the present and made explicit by the arrival of *The Lights*, namely, how to evaluate poems by a writer whose works flicker between prose and poetry. This problematic—how the formal integument of writing does, or does not, define the prose/poetry opposition—has been of persistent interest to Lerner.

Take *Gold Custody*, for example. A 2021 collaboration with artist Barbara Bloom, this book of longer-than-prose-poems and photographic montages contributes nine items to *The Lights*, spread throughout in roughly the same order as before, forming the spinal column of that book

as it were. The first poem borrowed from *Gold Custody* begins:

> Imagine a song, she said, that gives voice to people's anger. These weren't her actual words. The anger precedes the song, she continued, but the song precedes the people, the people are back-formed from their singing, which socializes feeling, expands the domain of the feelable. The voice must be sung into existence, so song precedes speech, clears the ground for it. Then how are we speaking now, I asked, although not in those words.

"The Stone" teaches the reader how to read *The Lights*. As in some previous work of his, Lerner signals an ineluctable delay between lyric voice ("the song") and lyric subjectivity ("feeling"). Influenced by Allen Grossman's readings of Walt Whitman and Hart Crane, and Michael Clune's readings of John Keats's odes, Lerner has long been fascinated by the incapacity of poetic language to actualize the literary and social values it nevertheless conveys. What Grossman says of Whitman and Crane or Clune of Keats, Lerner implies of himself. On this basis, the Lerner poem will be missing in action, locatable in some strange way on another plane of existence from the words on the page ("although not in those words") or the voice hanging in the air ("The voice must be sung into existence"). That is how one could understand the use of prose for "The Stone" and the rest of the *Gold Custody* group, which collectively push the limits of the prose poem form. They are poems in prose, inferentially, because that is more honest clothing for actual poetry than the meretricious cuts of lineation.

"Auto-Tune," a poem-poem that Lerner place immediately after "The Stone" in *The Lights*, get at the same poetics of deferral through its discussion of the phase vocoder, Bede's famous narrative of Cædmon ("His withdrawing...is the founding moment of English poetry," write Lerner), and environmental destruction in the Anthropocene. Cædmon comes up again and again in *The Lights*, though never by name: "it time / To write the first poem in English / Each line the last," Lerner commands in "The Pistil Here again Lerner translates the critical intona tions of Grossman's *The Long Schoolroom: Lessons* the Bitter Logic of the Poetic Principle into imaginative writing. (Lerner's *The Hatred of Poetry*, somewhat less comfortably, had attempted to retranslate in the other direction, from bitter poetry back toward didactic prose). "Auto-Tune" dreams "A dream in prose of poetry, a long dream of waking." The poem's lines are so long they verge on prose rhythm, but lineation relieves them nonetheless, lending a different edge to the "dream in prose of poetry" from the discussion of song in "The Stone." If *The Lights* has a manifesto, it is "Auto-Tune."

One could come to the same conclusion by reading *The Lights* archaeologically. "Auto-Tune" was first published in *BOMB* back in 2010, making it the oldest poem in the book. Lerner has scarcely changed a word, just cleaning up an obvious error ("This the" in *BOMB* becomes "This is the" in *The Lights*) and deleting "It is" from the last line ("It is a dream in prose . . ." becomes "A dream in prose . . ."). It is a feature of *The Lights*, in fact, that all the poems in it previously appeared elsewhere, in books or magazines, in identical or closely similar form. This is a remarkable professional choice and calls for comment. To a reader who has been following Lerner's career carefully, the book gives the impression of self-curation. More so than in the 2000s, when he was putting out books of poems at a clip of one every couple of years, Lerner reveals himself to be parsimonious with his own authorial labor. No poetic motion shall go wasted. All four poems in *No Art* that were new then, that is, those postdating the poetic trilogy, are recycled for *The Lights*, and in the same order as before. The two books share the same opening and closing poems, "Index of Themes" and "No Art" respectively, with not a single word changed. In *No Art*, "Index of Themes" indexes Lerner's collected poetic corpus up to that point, 2016. Seven years on, the identical poem comes to introduce and frame the previously uncollected work in the reader's hands: *The Lights*, one element in what one can only imagine will become a second poetic trilogy. "Index of Themes" may have suggested Lerner's title, since the final stanza, most appropriately to this book, mentions "a serial work about lights." If in drawing

together *No Art* Lerner suggested how poetic form could compose a career, in *The Lights* the career decomposes back into constituent forms, prose and verse. "I completed my study of form // and forgot it." "Poems about you, prose / poems." These passages come from "Index of Themes," but their point is sharpened in *The Lights* in view of the prominence in that book of uncomfortably long prose poetry and their subtextual reference to Lerner's intervening novels. More cynically, you could say that *The Lights* supplants *No Art* as the summative statement of Lerner's poetics, one book substituted for three.

Speaking of trilogies, *The Lights* bewrays an obsession with threes, from "Untitled (Triptych)" to the tripartite "Dilation," "The Circuit," and "The Rose," (the second poem of that title). The last of these miniaturizes Lerner's career to date in that part 1 is poetry, part 2 is prose, and part 3 returns to poetry. Each part of "The Rose" occupies a single page opening, a symmetry Lerner surely planned for. Thesis, antithesis, synthesis. "The ideal is visible through its antithesis like small regions of warm blue underpainting," muses the third movement of "Dilation," evoking medieval and Renaissance overpainted triptychs. Or it is like one of those high-school math puzzles. Identify the next number in the series: poetry, prose, ____. Like Anne Carson, Lerner overtly writes toward an unknown and unnamable genre, but one that will—as in part 3 of "The Rose"—sound a whole lot like poetry to most readers. One passage in "Untitled (Triptych)" says as much, with an allusion back to "Auto-Tune" and Cædmon:

> Here I am
> mitering two dreams: the dream of the poem,
> then the dream of the poem of that dream,
> the one you write on waking, publish in
> a limited edition with abundant color plates, but
> you can't really join them, the dreams,
> not without their collapsing into prose, so
> you write two novels, waiting for results
> it might be necessary to work back from.

In the version published earlier in *Harper's*, Lerner had "*Lana Turner* or *The Paris Review*" for "a limited edition with abundant color plates," so that in revision he has nudged the line from particularity to generality and across artistic media. At the time that he composed "Untitled (Triptych)," which appeared in 2015, Lerner had written two novels. Including the poem in *The Lights* without emending "two novels" to "three novels," even amid other touch-ups, suggests an act of self-historicization, a moment caught in amber that cannot be messed with. But equally, Lerner draws forward that understanding past the career moment on which it had been commenting in 2015. The quoted passage intimates that Lerner understood then, and understands now, his oscillation between the two major forms of contemporary literature to be not so much the prodigious accomplishment that it is as a form of genre desperation: "you write two novels, waiting . . ." Waiting for a form that could redeem the poetry/prose antinomy. "The problem is how to deliver the news / in a form that dissolves it into feeling," he writes, a few pages later, and this use of *dissolves* connects, chronologically and thematically, to the novel that dissolves into a poem in *10:04*. "Untitled (Triptych)" is precisely as long and just as resonant as "The Dark Threw Patches Down upon Me Also," with lines of a similar length. Placement of the two poems in *The Lights* is symmetrical, with approximately the same number of pages and poems preceding "The Dark" toward the beginning of the book as succeed "Untitled" toward the end. From these and other indications, I venture that Lerner wrote "Untitled" and "The Dark" as companion pieces or mirror images of one another, *circa* 2014. "Untitled" is a miniaturized novel in verse, this time shorn of the surrounding novel. It has a close cousin in the shorter and slightly earlier "Rotation," also included in *The Lights*.

In effect—and perhaps inevitably—*The Lights* readies Lerner's poetry for those many new readers that his novels have won him, readers not necessarily enrolled in the internecine debates in poetry-writing circles about accessibility, avant-gardism, and lyric form. The recycling of the *No Art* poems as well as the use of character vignettes in the *Gold Custody* pieces in prose express an intention to address a newfound public. Most telling in this regard is "The Readers," a *Paris Review* poem that meditates on (Lerner's) children as a new obligatory readership that pressurizes poetry:

> the voice that is
> mine only in part must be kept
> safe from them. They are too trivial
> my offices, too intimate, it isn't labor
> I cannot bring my daughters to work
>
> or not bring them
> here. They have learned to pause
> at the end of lines . . .

The risk associated with addressing neophyte readers reverberates backwards and forwards through the book's many discussions of poetic voice, labor, and authorial status ("my offices"), catalyzing the whole project. "The Readers," in other words, is another manifesto. It articulates the rhetorical quandary that Lerner identified, in a December 2022 appearance at Harvard University, as the problem inspiring *The Lights*. That is the appearance of the writer's own children as prospective readers of his work. The wry title "The Readers" in tandem with the conclusion of "Untitled (Triptych)" ("a friend of my / daughters' is how I think of you, reading / a poem you're on both sides of") denominate readers of *The Lights* into Lerner's family, a gesture of intimacy/patronage whose simultaneous aggression is not lost on him.

"The Camperdown Elm," another *Paris Review* poem, similarly attempts to see poetry and poetry writing through a child's eyes. It plays the same dissonant chord of violence underneath domesticity:

> I place a firefly in each cup
> I place them in the branches of
> And ask it to watch over her
>
> . . .
>                    slow
>
> Pulse of it, the intervals
> Shorter on warm nights, it won't
> Kill you, the pathetic fallacy
> My August fallacy, so that fall
> So that September has a flaw
> In the glass of it, where it catches, is
> Damaged lightly and released.

The almost obnoxiously Keatsian imagery (elm, autumn, nighttime) belies the closing inversion, whereby scene and season themselves become trapped, like fireflies, in glass or in child's hands. For Keats's "thou hast thy music too," said of autumn, Lerner substitutes "September has a flaw / In the glass of it," maybe the loveliest lines in *The Lights*. Poetry has a flaw in the glass of it. Fireflies are something of a signature image for Lerner's thought about the affordances of artistic form. Their crushed abdomens supplied glowing mush for eyeblack in his first book, *The Lichtenberg Figures*. (In a 2014 interview with Tao Lin, Lerner incidentally mentioned that that image came to him in a "recurring dream.") One live firefly crashes an outdoor opera in *The Hatred of Poetry*. In "The Camperdown Elm," Lerner indulges in the pathetic fallacy and then puts the pathetic fallacy itself under glass, another specimen in preparation for a more scientific—and therefore brutal—taxonomy of forms. The poem achieves all this through simple language, language a young daughter could understand. It is not a poem you have to puzzle over much.

So Lerner's poetic voice has become ever more inviting, ever more willing to defuse the difficult surface effects of the avant-garde styles in which he was trained. Readers coming to his poetry for the first time now nevertheless will be challenged. The title poem, another triptych, draws forward into *The Lights* a trick Lerner had perfected in *Mean Free Path*, whereby the line break frequently marks an otherwise unannounced break in sense:

> I think it is ok to want that, that wrong desire
> must have its place in your art, that the trails
> ice probably, and we are alone
> and we are not alone with being
> Out for the first time since the pandemic, we
>     fought
> about the dog and who is allowed to use the word
> "Palestine," and then almost made up about how
> the insolubility, how every problem
> scales, and I made my joke
> which is not a joke, about the leaked footage
> our only hope. Is the work
> to get outside the logic of solution or to work
> as if there were one, ones
>
> among us. I'm sure they are almost all military.

The poem first appeared in the *New York Review of Books*, in precisely the same form as here. Lerner experiments with what scholars term the construction *apo koinou*. Thus "wrong desire" is held in common between two incompatible syntaxes, "I think it is ok to want that, that wrong desire" and "wrong desire / must have its place in your art." The clause "Out for the first time" continues the previous line ("we are not alone with being") but also begins an unrelated period, as the capital *O* indicates. In both cases, the line break is a hiccup dividing two construals. "The Lights" situates the same Lerneresque worries about "the work" of poetry in the unlikely interval between the sighting of an unidentified flying object and the provision of a mundane explanation for it (contrails, Russian aircraft, US military). That peculiar temporal suspension becomes an evocative metaphor for the expectancy that Lerner's formal play broaches, an interstitial moment after cognition but prior to any of the rationalizations of recognition, after experience but before the analysis of experience, after one line but before the next. The discordant syntax of the poem ("her white dress stood out against the dark gray / sudden drop in pressure") reperforms what its metastasizing images of lights, sky, and sculpture suggest on another level.

Likewise drawn forward from *Mean Free Path*, thus picking up where Lerner had left off in poetry, is an oblique affirmation of John Stuart Mill's definition of poetry. "Eloquence is *heard*, poetry is *over*heard," wrote Mill. "Eloquence supposes an audience; the peculiarity of poetry appears to us to lie in the poet's utter unconsciousness of a listener. Poetry is feeling, confessing itself to itself in moments of solitude... All poetry is of the nature of soliloquy." Lerner activates this famous passage in "Meridian Response," another *New York Review of Books* poem, which he places immediately after "The Lights":

> experiments in hearing
> *as*: distortion *as*
> music, ocean *as* traffic, wind in the trees
>     like overheard
> speech. The not yet audible sound of me
>     clinging to belief.

In addition to the echoes of Mill, who equated poetry to overheard speech, and Ludwig Wittgenstein, who theorized "seeing as," Lerner picks up one thread of *Mean Free Path*. In a section of that fugue-like work, he likened April to "overheard speech" and imagined "interference heard as music." The same phrase and the same simile from "Meridian Response" echoes in "The Son," a poem from *Gold Custody* placed near the end of *The Lights*: "Wind in the poplars, overheard speech, traffic noise." At worst, such repetitions turn merely repetitious. They suggest an author struggling to break out of a small set of compulsive thought-patterns and points of reference. But at best repetition of image and thought lends a deal of coherence to a book that lacks a single, unifying formal gesture, something no component of Lerner's poetic trilogy lacked. Mostly, *The Lights* works. The many echoes between the poems are very carefully spaced (this being the real work of constructing the book, whose component poems all existed already).

The conversation about perception between *Mean Free Path* and *The Lights* goes, again, to the big question of form, of whether form is something to which you can return. If hearing distortion as music is or were humanly possible, then neither music nor distortion could sound the same again. Interpreted by the light of the hallucinatory lines "distortion *as* / music, ocean *as* traffic," Lerner's characteristic poetic moment would have the status of a crystalline melodic flourish piercing the pulverous atmosphere of a distorted musical composition, as if a snatch of Vivaldi had interrupted a Nirvana song. In a re-

view of *Mean Free Path* for *Jacket*, David Gorin perceptively saw the interference passages in that book expressing the experiences of

> a teenager in the 1980s and 90s...listening to punk, post-punk, grunge, industrial, and glitch, in which musicians deliberately interfered with the transmission of clean signals—using distorted guitars, feedback, lo-fi recordings, poorly-tuned instruments, and screamed or mumbled vocals drowned under a wash of sound—to project a dirty music.

Lerner was born in 1979. Of the musical genres Gorin lists, grunge is the best atmospheric fit for Lerner's aesthetic. He is the Kurt Cobain of contemporary poetry. Since *Mean Free Path*, Lerner hasn't stopped wondering how to use distortion to dirty up a poem. In some sense—a sense hidden from readers who know him only as a novelist, or, as at a recent lecture hosted by a discussion group from Boston College's education school, not even as a novelist but as a cultural critic—Lerner's novels themselves became fuel for that fire. At least, that is the implication of *The Lights*. But the result of the conflagration of available literary forms would be a new synthesis among them. To switch from a stationary to a mobile metaphor, Lerner writes toward a future in which poem and novel will have receded together in the rearview mirror of his literary vehicle, equally minuscule and now indistinguishable.

---

**REVIEW** | Sarah Manvel

*The Education of Crazy Jane*
Steven B. Sandler
self-published, 2024

I n the same way that an immortal American archetype is that of the cowboy of the old west, the modern archetypal equivalent is that of the hippie. A hippie might even be a stronger American stereotype as it is gender-neutral. Both men and women were full participants of the flower power movement of the late 1960s, tuning in, turning on and dropping out,

and the idea of the hippie, especially in conflict with traditional power sources, has powered countless American stories. *The Education of Crazy Jane*, self-published by Steven B. Sandler, is another one of them, although the noisy title is misleading. This tale of protest and disillusionment among college students in Michigan, light and fast-paced read, is less about what one woman learns and more about what one young man wants her to know.

It's 1968 and Jane Adagio is active in the SDS and studying to be a painter while her older brother Anthony has enlisted in the army for tour in Vietnam. Anthony has three inseparable childhood friends—Matt, a stoner musician, Trotsky, a political firebrand with beard and glasses, and Sam, a mild-mannered history student—who live together in a shared house while they study and, more importantly to them, figure out their own opinions about the political moment. Jane knows her own mind and is more interested in bringing the lads around to her point of view. The lads are more moderate, to an extent. They do a large amount of their own cooking, and while they are doing their best not to be sexist their actions (and their willingness to label Jane 'crazy' among many other things) make it clear that they are not interested in having any woman do their thinking for them.

At first Sam has a stridently feminist girlfriend named Suzanne he doesn't much like. He meets Jane for the first time in years when she puts herself in harm's way at a protest to retrieve an heirloom watch he'd dropped. This impresses Sam, but not for the right reasons; although he'd never say it, he prefers a woman who puts him first. The way Mr Sandler repeatedly contrasts Suzanne's tone-policing-as-activism with Jane's easygoing but serious willingness to break the law for the greater good makes this extremely clear. And yet when Jane and Sam become a serious couple, an awful lot of energy is devoted to Sam's feelings about Jane's protest work. You can tell a man wrote this because his ability to imagine a young woman's life is entirely limited to her interactions with men. Jane paints, makes macrame plantholders, designs anti-war -shirts, and has bottomless energy to join campus gatherings, but while the boys have each other she only has Sam. Other than the time she spends with her brother, her boyfriend and his housemates, none of Jane's other relationships are shown. No female friends coming round, no cups of coffee with an aunt.

But if the book is that classic masculine fantasy of a strong woman being brought to heel for her own good, it is both gentler and less offensive than that description makes it sound. Jane's heedless willingness to throw herself into the fray for a cause has serious academic and legal consequences, and Sam's concern for her is equally for his comfort and her safety.

All the while they walked and talked, Sam was listening, considering, evaluating her positions on things. He didn't see her as ridiculous, of course. Naive, yes, but never ridiculous. If anything, he had put her on a pedestal. He was, we must remember, in love—a state of mind that often disregards the most obvious signs of excess, deficit or imperfection of any kind. Still, it was a stretch for him to embrace her Quixotic notions about the evolution of humanity. Well, he reasoned, if Jane was Quixotic in her ideals, then so was [leader of the Prague Spring] Mr Dubček. Besides, he definitely admired her for being bold enough to maintain such a glorious view, realistic or not.

Sam's ride-or-die childhood friendship with Anthony is also part of it. Jane sees her political actions as essential to helping her brother come home, though Anthony takes them as insults and expresses these feelings in regular letters to Sam, who feels caught between the rock of his personal ethos and the hard place of wanting to be a good boyfriend and friend. There must be a middle way between Anthony's war service and Jane's penchant for mayhem, but Sam can't quite find it. And when Anthony does come back from his tour, things become more complicated still.

There are some quirky narrative digressions than a more traditionally edited book would have lost, which would have been a shame. These diversions (which, very unusually, are not overdone) actually add to the bigger picture, which for all Sam and Jane's news interest and debate about the Prague Spring, they simply don't stop to see. They are young and in love, convinced of their own righteousness, and further convinced others will come around to their way of thinking. It's this evocation of the certainty of youth which is Mr Sandler's most significant achievement, and the reason *The Education of Crazy Jane* deserves an audience. Things have changed a great deal since 1968, but not everything, and it's useful to read stories like this to understand where the needle has moved, and why.

# Music on Recording: Lucia Dlugoszewski

Out of the blue an agreeable shock—a promotional email from Klangforum Wien announcing a release on two col legno CDs of the music of Lucia Dlugoszewski, seven works in all. Lucia died in 2000. Your very old reporter's crumbling memory puts our friendship's beginning at, perhaps, 1996. I'd acquired about a year earlier a review set of VoxBox CDs, *Orchestra of Our Time*, a program of classical's modernists—Arnold Schoenberg, Luigi Dallapiccola, George Crumb, Pierre Boulez, Henri Pousseur, Luciano Berio's treatment of Kurt Weill's *Surabaya Johnny*, and, to me, an unknown, Lucia Dlugoszewski.

But first, an inappropriate aside about recording, the impressions it imparts, and a confession: I am an audiophile. I wouldn't be surprised to learn that the *Diagnostic and Statistical Manual of Mental Disorders* lists audiophilia among other hobbies such as necrophilia, coprophilia and pedophilia. It shares features with religious mania. Or think, perhaps, of the insights one discovers in a First Nation sweat lodge. In matters of recorded sound an audiophile obsesses over anything relating to his playback array and is willing to spend inordinately in achieving an auditory Will-o'-the-Wisp. The farthest gone among us can drop several hundred K on electronics and mechanicals, and as much on cabling as buys a lightly used Ford F-150. The price of a pair of speakers can exceed that of a middling hamlet's operating budget. Certain turntable-tonearm rigs remind one of Rube Goldberg in a tidier frame of mind. There exists, I'm not kidding, a turntable-tonearm combo that costs a half-million. An audiophile professes to hear differences in electrical outlets. Mine are Japanese. We move on:

Audiophilia's gentry understands that music, more especially classical, is performed (mainly) by acoustic instruments. The best recordings capture a performance in as lifelike a manner as production hardware, one's playback system and room acoustics permit. One could call it a bug-in-amber idealization of a composer's creation—exquisite and permanent. The most lifelike recordings, in this listener's estimation, are minimalist, which is to say, accomplished with a lesser amount recording-site hardware, microphones and mixers especially. The VoxBox pair, released in 1995, was produced over the years by Marc Aubort and Joanna Nickrenz. As a reviewer in the main of twentieth-century classical on disc, my initial ho-hum interest in a bargain label's program differed little from review CDs I received routinely. My respiration accelerated on discovering that Aubort and Nickrenz's Elite Recordings, Inc. did the tech work.

The VoxBox's *Fire Fragile Flight*, with Joel Thome conducting the Orchestra of Our Time, comes in at 8:34. The col legno's, with Klangforum Wien conducted by Johannes Kalitzke, runs 11:13. That's a significant difference. I find it difficult to identify the disparities in a work consisting more of assertive shards than an articulated narration. Both recordings are superb. (The entirety of the col legno set is very well recorded.) Aubort's signature technique puts *Fire Fragile Flight* in an airier space. The col legno's presentation is more front-and-center—indeed, in-your-face—which is entirely appropriate for Lucy's energetic, often rambunctious music. Feldman wanted his music played quietly. Lucy, not.

As a generality (my go-to gambit), an avant garde's side-effect is often alienation. How difficult now to understand how the French Impressionists provoked consternation. Closer to our time, we've Jackson Pollock. ("My kid could do that!") Music lovers also require time to adapt, if ever. The fissure separating Braham from Webern is vast, and remains so. Lucy's intrusions place her in the New York School's wide net, which, in music, mostly meant John Cage and Morton Feldman. She'd studied with Cage and Edgar Varèse. The latter's exuberant aesthetic clearly carried the field. Lucy ascribed he failure to enter Cage-Feldman's inner sanctum to Feldman's hostility, touched with misogyny. Maybe so. Yet, from where I listen these many years on, there's more to it than animus. Their music, Cage's included, is poles apart. Feldman's musical language would never frighten small children or horses. His challenge to complaisance consists of the demands he makes on the listener's time. He wrote a string quartet that, if played without breaks, requires of its performers diapers, catheters or extraordinarily elastic bladders, which is why Feldman on recording is so much more enjoyable—one indeed takes breaks or merely plays a side or two. Further, a fine recording's eerily pristine setting betters that of live performance, especially in Feldman's case, in which a filigree creation occurs within a pitch-black silence. I have in mind a consistently superb Feldman project on Werner Uehlinger's HatArt label. Alas and alack, and woe is me, a ton of years ago I recommended Lucy's music to Uehlinger, unsuccessfully. These Klangforum Wien performances handsomely fill that void. So bravo col legno, the Polish Ministry of Culture and National Heritage, the Adam Mickiewicz Institute, and anything or anyone I've failed to mention.

Lucy was married to the dancer-choreographer Erick Hawkins, who died in 1994. She adored the man and his memory, which did not deter her from saying, I suspect, tongue-in-cheek, that she'd be hitting on me were it not for my Polish wife. Prim fellow that I am, I tried not to look shocked. Hawkins and his company figure large in Lucy's compositions. In the way of prestige, disc one begins with a work for trumpet and orchestra commissioned by trumpeter Gerard Schwartz and the New York Philharmonic when under Pierre Boulez' direction: *Abyss and Caress* (1975). Similarly, *Fire Fragile Flight* won a Koussevitsky International Recording Award in 1977. (This had to have been the Aubort-Nickrenz session.) The set's excellent German-English notes cover whatever you're likely to ask.

ALVIN KRINST

# The Fascino Fragments

*These tantalizing fragments are testaments to the untiring diligence of Krinst scholarship. Found in 2015 amongst a previously neglected trove of Krinst's papers that, disappointingly, was in deplorable condition and consisted mostly of restaurant receipts, commercial leaflets, and quotidian business correspondence, they might never have been noticed had not Institute of Krinst Studies Senior Fellow Jean-Paul Hogman, exhausted by the tedious work of sorting through the archive, tipped over a cup of lapsang souchong onto his cockapoo Foucault. In admirable haste to unscald the animal, Hogman used papers previously relegated to the wastebasket to sop up the burning liquid, and the hot moisture happened to dislodge a single handwritten sheet that, having adhered to an overdue bill from one Dr. Fascino, Krinst's dentist, had been mistakenly overlooked. Ignoring his pet's protests, Hogman slowly and carefully separated the valuable relic, and saw it contained two different, hitherto unknown Krinstian texts: a brief letter, full of imaginative biographical detail, drafted to an unknown correspondent named "Warren," and, on the other side, a paragraph clearly intended for his legendary novel* No Smoking, *in which the protagonist, Dlll, appears to be upset with the racket produced by nearby real estate developers (an annoyance with neighbors being almost as fertile a theme in Krinst's work as breakfast foods). Note that in the second fragment, as throughout the novel, Dlll's pronouns alternate genders, in strict sequence.*

—Walter Smart

## 1. Letter to "Warren"

My dearest "Warren":
Of course I remember you; how sly of you to imply that I might not, by suggesting that your memory of me might in turn be conceived of as mapped onto a domain of possibility that includes the perishable. You were always such a wag.

Those randy evenings in Budapest, when, after sharing a bottle of St. Hubertus, you extemporized in vilely accented mock Dutch on Spinoza's hypothetical body modifications while fondling a dachshund; your perhaps regrettable high spirits days later in the Sofia Hilton, when we doused the Spahi's rubber duckie with Courvoisier and set it afire, and enraged, he threatened to behead us; the ill-fated trek to return salt from Dandi to Sabarmati (you dismissed the problem of humidity—I told you we should have bought Morton's); the uncanny quiet and inviting darkness of the docks at night in Naples, in the crossed shadows of oil tankers; the hilarious evening in Dakar when Muhammed dared you to squat nude in a tub of harissa and I was bitten so inconveniently by his ape Bubbles. Certainly, we had our spats. I don't choose to dwell on your provocations. I admit that Everest was my low point; actually, I did not know until I got your letter that you had made it back to base camp.

Looking back on it all, however, all our excess and turpitude is somehow dissolved in a harmony, not resolved, but lingering with delicate straining dissonance in a longing satisfied best, though incompletely, by itself. Who could name it anything other than a success?

Little is new here. Due to the apocalyptic melting of the permafrost throughout the Arctic, my hut here in Karasjok has sunk six feet over the past two years, and I may be forced to relocate to Florence as I've been threatening for so long.

Don't hesitate to do anything, including hesitate.

As always—*AK*

## 2. "DLLL sat in shop . . ." (from *No Smoking*)

**D**lll sat in shop and cradled his spitto How squeaky, she reflected, the imperr nent racketeers could be in their rub-a-d dubbingly frightful blandishments. His wav ing ear accused the ephemeral cranks of highlands of saturating curved space w square waves and smoking ferrets in secret the distant fields beyond the barn, yellowing starchy clouds with their annoying counter surgencies. Hollering triumphal inaccurac with much gloating humph and broadly pas to-do, they muddily stamp after their scurry foes, devastating the valuable sod whose evac tion they madly envision will gratify their scra bled seats of satiety. Small bones suspended exquisitely sensitive fluid registered inside D by minute attention to thumps of no little quancy and their subtle variations and modu tions and the arabesques of frequency and a plitude therein, a heinous vibration radiat from a spiritual grossness, souring the inter lactic vacuum with an opprobrious ontism a rending the arbitrarily fine fabric so sublim inscribed in the jewel of the world by their b ters. High-pitched and inflexible denunciatic tumbled one after another into the multifaric sensibility aforementioned, by nature immu to their constant and grating appeals. Rath she furnished in the space of his thought ghastly chamber of recompense for these v lains, who there would meet the rewards ind ferent Fortuna seemed undisposed to mete c in the manifested surfaces of her fantasy.

CHRISTOPHER BOUCHER

# The Great Ungluing

The first reported episode of ungluing took place in 2020 and involved a University of Minnesota student named True Darry. Darry was walking through campus with her friend Rob L. Maze one afternoon that fall when Maze saw something fall from the book Darry was carrying—Maze said later he thought it was a bookmark—and alerted Darry. Darry said in a 2023 interview that she looked down at her feet and saw a sentence on the asphalt. "Are those *words*?" Maze reportedly said.

"I remember exactly what the words were, actually," Darry recalled in the interview.

"'To the gallop of four horses,' something something."

Neither of them thought much of it, nor did the school bookstore clerk when Darry returned the book that afternoon. Over the next few months, though, more reports of unstuck words emerged—not only in literature, but in newspapers, advertisements, legal contracts, white papers, menus, you name it. In one instance, for example, the slippage from an ingredients listing on a cereal box in Australia caused a consumer to have a violent allergic reaction. In another, two corporations in Qatar landed in court over language from one contract that fell into another.

An international investigation was launched the following spring, and the source of the problem soon discovered: A Baltimore-based company called Global Adhesives—the largest and oldest supplier of the proprietary glue that is mixed into all common inks—had been distributing faulty batches of its wordglue going back all the way to the 1990s. Global was aware of the faulty batches, as it turned out, but they'd chosen to keep it quiet and deal with affected clients individually. The problem was now too big to cover up, though, the bad glue too wide-spread. Global immediately removed the faulty formula from the market, but the damage was already done.

Without a feasible way to discern the words that would stick from those that wouldn't, the world fell into chaos. Everywhere you read, words fell out of place—dropping out of books or, in some cases, falling through a book or from one book to another. Countless businesses closed, including several major presses, many bookstores and most news kiosks. In schools and restaurants, meanwhile, a new emphasis was placed on the spoken word; waiters would often recite the menu to you, for example.

We certainly felt the effect of the Great Ungluing over here at *Exacting Clam*. We were hard at work on Issue 14 at the time, and we were so paranoid about the movement of words that we hired a "wordguard"—a hermit crab named Pavel—to keep watch over the text. Pavel came highly recommended—he'd formerly been head of word security at Cordelia, Cordelia and Lone—but he turned out to be untrustworthy. One morning we found him fast asleep and snoring on the copyright page next to an empty six-pack of hard seltzers. About a week later, Pavel disappeared; he quit without telling anyone and wandered away.

As it turned out, though, ten crabs wouldn't have made a difference: the ungluing was rampant. One afternoon that fall, editor Crowd Billingsley was proofreading page 103 when she radioed in to report a missing sentence. We all flocked to the location—it was in the middle of an essay called "A Return to Form?"—to find Crowd standing in the space between two phrases, "with his own authorial labor" and "All four poems." "Wasn't there a sentence here?" Billingsley asked.

Someone checked the draft. Crowd was right; the sentence "No poetic motion shall go wasted." had gone missing. We spread out and looked around, and soon found that the sentence had unstuck and tumbled onto the next page, into an excerpt of cited verse that read, "Here I am / mitering two dreams..." Now the verse read, "Here I am no poem / mitering unwasted two dreams."

I helped Billingsley and two other editors carry the words back to their place. We hoped that might be the only incident of ungluing, but the next morning Mar Doyle radioed from a story called "Triptych-on-Sea" for help with a similar melding: two sentences, *"How do I go about adopting a retired greyhound"* and *"WHAT ARE THE FULL LYRICS TO I DO LIKE TO BE BESIDE THE SEASIDE"* had merged into "How do I go about adopting a FULL SEASIDE," while a word from another story had fallen to form "WHAT ARE THE LYRICS TO Bookcases?"

We were still trying to untangle those words when my colleague Kevin Fluke radioed from another essay. "Ow-eye ex," he shouted. "Ow-eye-ex!"

"Say again?" I hollered.

"Outside text!" Kevin repeated.

Several of us left Doyle and ran over to page 4, and what we saw there took my breath away. Kevin was kneeling next to a sentence that read,

"I'm reminded of the story about the French philosopher *As I Lay Dying* coming back from the tea-break..."

"That should be 'Derrida!'" spat Fort Belieu, who'd helped set the essay on the page. "Where is 'Derrida'? Has anyone seen 'Derrida'?"

"Derrida" was missing for two days —we looked everywhere for it. And where did we find it? Not in the issue, but on the bookshelf in the office, on the spine of another book, which now read: *Derrida, Newburyport.*

It took months for Global Adhesives to issue a fix. The following summer they distributed a lacquer that, when applied to a word, would affix it to its surface (though it left them with a burnt-orange tint—you could always spot a re-glued word).

I couldn't even write that, though—couldn't even conclude my story "The Great Ungluing." Everytime I tried to add an ending, the words

kept

oh no

stay

with

me,

words!

The Left Hand

Oh how

did

of

The words

kept

Darkness

falling—

*EXACTING CLA*

# Contributors

**César Dávila Andrade** (Cuenca, 1918—Caracas, 1967) was an Ecuadorian poet, short fiction writer, and essayist. He was known as El Fakir for both his physical appearance and the mystical and esoteric concerns of his work. His chronicle of atrocities and forced labor under Spanish rule, "Bulletin and Elegy of the Mitas," is widely acclaimed, both critically and popularly, as a key text of 20th century Ecuadorian poetry.

**Terena Elizabeth Bell** is the author of a short story collection, *Tell Me What You See* (Whiskey Tit, 2022). Her writing has appeared in many publications, including *The Atlantic, Playboy, MysteryTribune*, and *Santa Monica Review*. A Sinking Fork, Kentucky native, she lives in New York City.

**Jesi Bender** is an artist from Upstate New York. She helms KERNPUNKT Press, a home for experimental writing. She is the author of *Dangerous Women* (dancing girl press, 2022), *KINDERKRANKENHAUS* (Sagging Meniscus, 2021) and *The Book of the Last Word* (Whiskey Tit 2019). Her shorter writing has appeared in *The Rumpus, Split Lip, Adroit Journal*, and elsewhere.

**Israel A. Bonilla** lives in Guadalajara, Jalisco. He is author of the micro-chapbook *Landscapes* (Ghost City Press, 2021). His work has appeared in *Your Impossible Voice, Firmament, Minor Literature[s], Berfrois, King Ludd's Rag*, and elsewhere. *Sleep Decades*, his debut short story collection, is forthcoming from Malarkey Books (2024).

**Christopher Boucher** is the author of the novels *How to Keep Your Volkswagen Alive* (Melville House, 2011), *Golden Delicious* (MH, 2016), and *Big Giant Floating Head* (MH, 2019). He teaches writing and literature at Boston College and is Managing Editor of *Post Road Magazine*.

**Ian Boulton** is a former community mobilisation consultant who has worked extensively in Russia, Ukraine and many of the countries that made up the former Soviet Union. Now he lives in the UK and writes short fiction.

**Oisín Breen** is published in 121 journals in 22 countries, including *Agenda, NDQ, Books Ireland, Southward* and *Quadrant*. Breen has two collections, *Lilies on the Deathbed of Étaín*, a Scotsman book-of-the-year, 2023 (Downingfield), and *Flowers, All Sorts, in Blossom...* (Dreich, 2020). Breen's third, *The Kergyma*, is due 2025 (Salmon).

**Yoo Chiwhan** (1908–1967) was a leading Korean poet. In English, see *Blue Stallion: Poems of Yu Chi-whan* (trans.Sung-Il Lee, Homa & Sekey Books, 2011).

**Kim Chunsu** (1922–2004) was one of the leading South Korean poets of the late twentieth century. A selection of his work is available in English, translated by Kim Jong-Gil: *The Snow Falling on Chagall's Village* (Cornell University Press, 2010).

**Marvin Cohen** is the author of many novels, plays, and collections of essays, stories, and poems. He lives on the Lower East Side of Manhattan.

**Yoon DongJoo** (1917–1945), a poet active in the Korean independence movement, died at age 27 in a Japanese prison, possibly as a result of medical experimentation. His poetry, published posthumously, is highly prized in Korea and beyond. In English, see *Sky, Wind and Stars* (tran. Kyung-nyun Kim Richard and Steffen F. Richards, Asian Humanities Press, 2003).

**Sean Ennis** is the author of *Cunning, Baffling, Powerful* (Thirty West). He lives in Mississippi and more of his work can be found at seanennis.net.

**Julian George**'s work has appeared in *the Naugatuck River Review, Perfect Sound Forever, New World Writing, Slag Glass City, Panoplyzine, Ambit, The Journal of Music, Film Comment, The London Magazine, Cineaste* and *Art Review*. His novel, *Bebe*, is out now in CB Editions. He Zooms on jazz for Open Age.

**Laura Givens** is based in Kansas City, Missouri. She has worked a variety of jobs, including house painter, barista, union organizer, and civil servant.

**Jake Goldsmith** is a writer with cystic fibrosis and the founder of The Barbellion Prize, a book prize for ill and disabled authors. He is the author of *Neither Weak Nor Obtuse* (SM, 2022) and *In Hospital Environments: Essays on Illness and Philosophy* (SM, 2024).

**Abbie Hart** (she/they) is a 20-year-old poet from Houston, TX currently living in Worcester, MA. She has been published over 30 times, and is the editor in chief for the *Literary Forest Poetry Magazine*. Her first chapbook, *head is a home*, is forthcoming through Bottlecap Press.

**John Patrick Higgins** is the author of *Teeth* (SM, 2024) and *Fine* (SM, 2024). He lives in Belfast.

**Charles Holdefer** lives in Brussels. His latest book is *Ivan the Terrible Goes to a Family Picnic* (SM, 2024).

**Nick Holdstock** is the author of two novels, *The Casualties* (St Martins, 2015) and *Quarantine* (Swift, 2022), and a short story collection, *The False River* (Unthank, 2019). He has written three non-fiction books about China: *The Tree That Bleeds* (Luath, 2012), *Chasing the Chinese Dream* (IB Tauris, 2017) and *China's Forgotten People* (Bloomsbury, 2019).

**Richard Kostelanetz** is an American writer, artist, critic, and editor of the avant-garde. He survives in New York, where he was born, unemployed and thus overworked.

**Alvin Krinst** is the author of *The Yalta Stunts* (SM, 2016), a translation of Dante's *Inferno* (into limericks), the novel *No Smoking*, the poetry collection *GIGFY*, the ballet *The Jazz Age of Haroun Al-Rashid*, and many other works. He divides his time between Quito, Ecuador and Reykjavík, Iceland.

**Jake La Botz**'s songs and acting have been featured in film and television, including *True Detective*, *Shameless*, *Ghost World*, *Rambo* (yes, *Rambo*!) and more. His debut collection of short fiction is forthcoming from the University of Wisconsin's Cornerstone Press.

**Roy Lisker** (1938–2019) was a writer, artist, mathematician, journalist and political activist. He was the author of a vast amount of literature in every imaginable form, which he largely self-distributed to friends and subscribers to his newsletter, *Ferment*. His conventionally published work includes *In Memoriam Einstein* (SM, 2016) and *Lincoln Center in July* (SM, 2016).

**Qianqian Liu** is an interdisciplinary artist based in Chicago. Qianqian is interested in temporalities and divergent becomings. Her work delves into the poetics of the overlooked and the inexplicable through humorous gestures that celebrate the intricacies of the mundane, the periphery, and the failed. Her book, *How to Make Imaginary Friends by Territorialization and Deterritorialization* (2024), is collected by the Joan Flasch Artists' Book Collection.

**Kurt Luchs** is the author of *Falling in the Direction of Up* (SM, 2020), *One of These Things Is Not Like the Other* (Finishing Line Press, 2019), and the humor collection *It's Funny Until Someone Loses an Eye (Then It's Really Funny)* (SM, 2017). He lives in Michigan.

**Sarah Manvel** is the author of *You Ruin It When You Talk* (Open Pen, 2020) as well as three other novels seeking a home. She is also a book, film and art critic for outlets including *Critic's Notebook*, *In Their Own League*, *Bookmunch* and *Minor Literature[s]*. A dual Irish-American national, she lives in London.

**Melissa McCarthy** transmits from a tracking station in Edinburgh, Scotland. She's written *Photo, Phyto,* *Proto, Nitro* (SM, 2023) and *Sharks, Death, Surfers: An Illustrated Companion* (Sternberg, 2019). She's fond of Melville. See sharksillustrated.org for more.

**Adam McPhee** is a Canadian writer whose words have appeared in venues such as *Old Moon Quarterly*, *Heavy Feather Review*, and *Ahoy Comics*. He has been longlisted for the CBC Short Story Prize and writes a newsletter, Adam's Notes, on Substack. He lives in Alberta.

**Juhan Oh** is an 8th-grade student in Seoul, Korea with a passion for translating Korean poetry.

**Eric T. Racher** lives and works in Riga, Latvia. He is the author of a poetry chapbook, *Five Functions Defined on Experience: For Jay Wright* (2021).

**Johnny White Really-Really** is a writer and comedian and musician and receptionist from Sheffield who lives in London. His recent show "Catland" got five stars in *Chortle*, if that means anything at all to you.

**Nicole Ricci** is an author and graphic designer based in New Jersey. More at nriccidesign.com.

**Mike Silverton** is the author of *Anvil on a Shoestring* (SM, 2022), *Trios* (SM, 2023) and *Yoga for Pickpockets* (SM, 2024). He lives in Maine.

**Jonathan Simkins** is the translator of *El Creacionismo* by Vicente Huidobro. His translations of César Dávila Andrade have appeared in *ballast, Bennington Review, Chicago Review, Interim, The Journal, Los Angeles Review, Modern Poetry in Translation*, and others. His fiction has appeared in *Bristol Noir, Close To The Bone*, and *Grim & Gilded*.

**Walter Smart** is a Senior Fellow at the Institute of Krinst Studies in Reykjavík, Iceland. He edited J.F Mamjjasond and Fafnir Finkelmeyer's *Hoptime* (SM 2017).

**Kim Sowol** (1902–1934) was a Korean poet. In English, see *Azaleas: A Book of Poems* (translated David R McCann, Columbia University Press, 2007).

**Thomas Walton** is the author of *Good Morning Bon Crusher!* (Spuyten Duyvil 2021), *All the Useless Things Ar Mine* (SM, 2020), *The World Is All That Does Befall U* (Ravenna Press, 2019), and, with Elizabeth Cooperman, *The Last Mosaic* (SM, 2018). He currently works a an AI yoga instructor at Ashram Deapphake in Seattle, WA.

**K Weber** lives and writes in southwestern Ohio. Mor at kweberandherwords.com.

**Eric Weiskott** is a poet and scholar of poetry and po etics. His poems appear in *Texas Review, Inverted Synta Versal*, and *Mudfish*. He lives in Massachusetts.